The LAUGHS On HOLLYWOOD

The LAUGHS On HOLLYWOOD

by
RICHARD WEBB
and
TEET CARLE

Illustrations by Bruce Pierce

ROUNDTABLE PUBLISHING, INC.
SANTA MONICA   CALIFORNIA

ROUNDTABLE PUBLISHING, INC.
933 Pico Boulevard
Santa Monica, CA 90405

First Printing, 1985

Library of Congress Catalog Card Number — 84-60760

Printed in the United States of America

Dedication

This volume is affectionately dedicated to all of the following, whose ability to laugh at themselves has allowed us to laugh along with them:

Joseph Agnello, Eddie and Margo Albert, Fred Allen, June Allyson, Carlton Andrews, Muriel Angelus, Cliff Arquette, Lady Sylvia Ashley, Fred Astaire, William Austin, George Axelrod, Arthur "Bugs" Baer, Fay Bainter, Lucille Ball, Tallulah Bankhead, Larry Barbier, Ethel Barrymore, John Barrymore, Warner Baxter, John Beck, Jack Benny, Solly Biano, Dorothy Black, Rufus Blair, Joan Blondell, Peter Bogdanovich, Frank Borzage, Clara Bow, William Boyd, Walter Bradfield, George Brown, Larry Buchanan, Sidney Buchman, Arthur Caeser, James Cagney, James Cain, MacDonald Carey, Walter Catlett, Jimmy Carter, Bennett Cerf, William Chapman, Charlie Chase, Maurice Chevalier, Steve Clensos, Harold Clurman, Irvin S. Cobb, Steve Cochran, Lew Cody, Harry Cohn, Jack Cohn, Claudette Colbert, Chester Conklin, Gary and Rocky Cooper, Harriet Coray, Jeff Corey, Joan Crawford, Laura Hope Crews, Bing Crosby, Michael Curtiz, Marion Davies, Bette Davis, Francisco "Chico" Day, Cecil B. DeMille, William Dieterle, Marlene Dietrich, Clint Eastwood, Thomas A. Edison, Jack Elam, John Engstead, Dave Epstein, Dutch Ergenbright, Douglas Fairbanks, Alice Faye, W.C. Fields, Eddie Fisher, Barry Fitzgerald, Errol Flynn, Henry Fonda, Bert Ford, John Ford, Gene Fowler, Will Fowler, Bryan Foy, Kay Francis, Lee Francis, Clark Gable, Eva Gabor, Gadabout Gaddis, Greta Garbo, Henry Ginsberg, George Glass, George Gobel, Paulette Goddard,

Samuel Goldwyn, Betty Grable, Ide Gruber, Leo Guild, Alan Hale, Sr., Robert Hammack, Oscar Hammerstein II, Dashiell Hammett, Merville Hammett, Oliver Hardy, Jean Harlow, Phil Harris, William Harris, William S. Hart, Sadakichi Hartman, Al Haskins, Henry Hathaway, Helen Hayes, Susan Hayward, Ben Hecht, Lillian Hellman, Jim Henaghan, Joseph Hill, Alfred Hitchcock, Phillips Holmes, Bob Hope, Hedda Hopper, James Wong Howe, George Hurrell, John Huston, Harold Huxley, Sam Jaffe, Arthur James, Allen Jenkins, Erskine Johnson, Al Jolson, Grover Jones, Hamilton Jordan, Jim Jordan, Jr., B.B. Kahane, Bernie Kamins, Mike Kaplan, Sam Katzman, Deborah Kerr, Michael Kidd, Barrett C. Kiesling, Clifton Kling, Norman Krasna, Veronica Lake, Hedy Lamarr, Glenn Langan, Oscar Lau, Stan Laurel, Paul Lavalle, D. Ross Lederman, Beatrice Lillie, Rich Little, Harold Lloyd, Clarence Locan, Carole Lombard, Myrna Loy, Alfred Lunt, Leo McCarey, Marie MacDonald, Kenneth McKenna, Fred MacMurray, Steve McQueen, Herman J. Mankiewicz, Fredric March, George Marion, Jr., Hazel Marshall, Pete Martin, Groucho Marx, Victor Mature, Jerry Mayer, Louis B. Mayer, Mary Mayer, Bill Meiklejohn, Adolph Menjou, Mary Miles Minter, Carmen Miranda, Robert Mitchum, Marilyn Monroe, Ricardo Montalban, Robert Montgomery, Kid Moreno, Frank Morgan, Zero Mostel, Florabel Muir, Ray Nazarro, Fairfax Nesbitt, Sir Laurence Olivier, Clifford Orr, William Orr, Maureen O'Sullivan, Debra Paget, Alexander Pantages, Dorothy Parker, Louella Parsons, Gregory Peck, Westbrook Pegler, Mary Pickford, Bill Pine, Lilly Pons, Cole Porter, Jody Powell, William Powell, Robert Preston, Aileen Pringle, Luise Rainer, Esther Ralston, Basil Rathbone, Ronald Reagan, Burt Reynolds, Frank Rich, Addison Richards, Hal Roach, John D. Rockefeller, Jr., Richard Rodgers, Roy Rogers, Cesar Romero, Mickey Rooney, Jane Russell, Rosalind Russell, Adolph L. "Whitey" Schafer, Carl Schroeder, David O. Selznick, Mack Sennett, Norma Shearer, Cybill Shepherd, Ann Sheridan, George Sherman, Harry "Pop" Sherman, Eddie Sieta, Beverly Sills, Allison Skipworth, Sidney Skolsky, Robert Slatzer, H. Allen Smith, Kate Smith, Jesse

Spiro, Barbara Stanwyck, John P. Stark, Adlai Stevenson, Sylvia Sydney, Norma Talmadge, Irving Thalberg, Bill Thomas, Mike Todd, Mel Torme, Lana Turner, Linn Unkefer, Lee Van Cleef, Lupe Velez, Charles Vidor, Josef Von Sternberg, Jerry Wald, Eli Wallach, Raoul Walsh, Jack Warner, Johnny Weissmuller, William Wellman, Mae West, Wally Westmore, Cornel Wilde, Billy Wilder, Bill Williams, Johnny Williams, Frank J. Wilstach, Grant Withers, Anna May Wong, Sam Wood, Teresa Wright, William Wyler, Herbert Yates, Robert Young, Darryl Zanuck, Adolph Zukor.

And all those unnamed directors, craftspersons, studio executives, actors and actresses, writers, and publicists who have permitted us to laugh with them over the years, but whose names have been omitted either through oversight or tact.

Acknowledgments

The authors wish to thank the many associates over many years who have shared laughs on Hollywood with us, including:

John Agar, Joseph Agnello, Richard Albain, Patti Andrews, Maxwell Arnow, Cliff Arquette, Robert Arthur, Gene Autry, John Barrymore, Solly Biano, Rufus Blair, Larry Buchanan, Carol Burnett, James Cagney, Harry Carey, Jr., MacDonald Carey, Steve Cochran, Tim Conway, Gary Cooper, Lou Costello, Bing Crosby, Michael Curtiz, "Chico" Day, James Dean, Nelson Eddy, Jack Elam, John Engstead, Eddie Fisher, Errol Flynn, Bert Ford, Will Fowler, Eva Gabor, Mitch Gamson, Tay Garnett, Sheridan Gibney, George Glass, George Gobel, Samuel Goldwyn, Leo Guild, Abe Haberman, Robert Hammack, Mabel Hill, Jack Hirshberg, Bob Hope, James Wong Howe, Ben Irwin, Ben Johnson, Erskine Johnson, Jim Jordan, Bernie Kamins, Mike Kaplan, Barrett Kiesling, Glenn Langan, D. Ross Lederman, Perry Leiber, Milt Lewis, Joe Louis, A.C. Lyles, Jeanette MacDonald, Ronald MacDougall, Hazel Marshall, Victor Mature, Mary Mayer, Bill Meiklejohn, Sid Melton, Irving Moore, Holly Morse, David Niven, Robert Preston, Leroy Prinz, Basil Rathbone, Addison Richards, Mickey Rooney, Oscar Rudolph, Russell Saunders, "Whitey" Schafer, Walter Seltzer, Robert Shawley, George Sherman, Robert Slatzer, Bill Thomas, Mel Torme, Coles Trapnell, Rudy Vallee, Lee Van Cleef, Clint Walker, Raoul Walsh, Ode Wannebo, John Wayne, Gene Webster, Johnny Weissmuller, Bill Williams, Grant Withers.

Contents

Introduction

by ROBERT OSBORNE

Is there anyone out there who doesn't have a favorite story about Hollywood? Its foibles and fantasies have helped elevate rumor-mongering to the level of being, perhaps, the eighth liveliest art.

There is the one, of course, about Louella Parsons, at one time Hollywood's most controversial (and, I might add, one of the industry's most supportive) chroniclers and gossip reporters. Louella was married to a doctor who liked his sauce after working hours. He also liked to play poker into the wee hours and, on a notable occasion, combined the two at a Sunday night party that was still continuing as the Monday morning sun came up. But when loyal Louella went to collect her doctor husband in order to wearily head home, he wasn't at the poker table, nor anywhere else to be found in their host's home. Panic time. Finally, all the remaining guests went on a frantic search and — viola! — found the doctor, dead drunk and passed out, face down near a water fountain far from the celebration. The discovery threw Louella into a momentary frenzy, and for good reason. "Help me wake him up!" she bellowed. "He has to perform a delicate surgery in one hour!"

Then there's the one about Cary Grant and a newspaper profiler. The New York newsman was writing a story on Grant and, needing some additional information for his story, he telegraphed Grant's Hollywood publicist. "How old Cary Grant?" was the message. By coincidence, Grant happened to be at the publicist's office when the wire arrived. He shot back a personal reply, also by telegraph. "Old Cary Grant fine. How you?"

Nothing gets excused from the catalog of Hollywood stories and folklore. People still love to tell how a bit of punctuation helped save a million-dollar investment on a Deanna Durbin film over at Universal Studios.

In the 1930s and 1940s, Deanna Durbin was an extremely important, and apparently guaranteed, box-office draw for her studio. There had been eight films, eight hits. Then, in 1940, she made number nine, a movie called *Nice Girl*. After previewing it, Universal's executives were jubilant. Durbin had obviously delivered hit number nine, a film that couldn't miss, shouldn't miss. But, curiously, when *Nice Girl* went into release, it didn't draw the customers. Disaster! The studio, initially distraught, then baffled, started doing some research.

What they discovered is that the title was too passive, too sweet, too unintriguing, especially when coupled with Durbin's own on-screen personna which was also unthreatening and squeaky clean. But the studio had already spent enough money pre-selling the title *Nice Girl*, they didn't want to scratch that handle altogether. It was the kind of catch-22 that can drive a person crazy. Or crazier.

Then some uncredited genius came up with a solution, one that didn't require a title change, intrigued the public into buying tickets to see the film, and turned the Durbin Number Nine into an immediate and substantial moneymaker. They simply added a question mark, and *Nice Girl* became *Nice Girl?*

Producer Samuel Goldwyn perhaps contributed more to Hollywood folklore than any other single individual, mainly due to his fracturing of English and sommersault phrases. (Although it should also be stated, adamantly, those often-quoted Goldwynisms never outweighed nor overshadowed his prowess as a producer. Enduring Goldwyn classics such as *Wuthering Heights*, *The Little Foxes*, *The Best Years of Our Lives*, *Ball of Fire*, and countless others attest to that.)

At one juncture, Goldwyn had under personal contract, among several, Merle Oberon and Miriam Hopkins, and he was constantly on the lookout for important stage or literary properties he could buy as possible screen vehicles for each lady.

One day he was talking by phone to a New York scout. Goldwyn asked, as he often did, if there was anything on the Broadway horizon that might be purchased as possible material for either Oberon or Hopkins. Negative. The New Yorker reported the Broadway action was slow at the moment, except for a new Lillian Hellman play called *The Children's Hour*. That play, indeed, contained not only a great role for Oberon but also one that would be ideal for Hopkins, a double whammy. "But Mr. Goldwyn, I don't think you'd be interested in it," said the scout. "Both of the women in the story are accused of being lesbians." Goldwyn didn't miss a beat. "Don't worry," he said enthusiastically. "For the movie, we can make them Americans!"

So it goes. The stories are endless, no subject or personality is sacred. Tales of Hollywood's leaders and its crackpots have been avalanching out to the far reaches of the world since Day One. Many of them, apparently, are either true or based in some truths — or now so ingrained in the folklore they might as well be. Who needs to make them up when there is so much rich, undiluted material out there?

There's only one problem. No one has ever bothered to put them all down on paper. We've had one-vision sprinklings from time to time, and some gorgeous stories verbalized in various biographies and autobiographies, but never a full-tilt, all-oars- ahead volume that's stitched those sagas under one set of book covers.

That's where I think Richard Webb and Teet Carle have done us a service. In *The Laughs on Hollywood*, they've collected a grand patch-quilt of great Hollywood stories, some of which I recognized with affection, many of which I'd never heard before.

Understandably, they haven't been able to include *all* the tales out there. If they had, there would be a volume so large that *Encyclopedia Britannica* salesmen would have to sell it in pieces, door to door, for payments of $50 monthly.

No postman, and no reader, would be able to lift the packet all the stories would require.

Mr. Webb and Mr. Carle had to start somewhere. I just hope it's the start of a trend, and the beginning of a series.

★ ★ ★

Robert Osborne is a columnist-critic for *The Hollywood Reporter*, and the author of eight books on the motion picture industry, including his award-winning *50 Golden Years of Oscar*, the only official biography of the Academy of Motion Picture Arts and Sciences.

The LAUGHS On HOLLYWOOD

I
TITLES

"My kingdom for a title!"

★ ★ ★

Before the advent of Edison's little invention, the "motion picture," the first elaborate Broadway "leg show" in America was the great epic, *The Black Crook*. The entertainment enjoyed a 15-month run in New York in 1866-67. (At the time, that was a long run.) Each performance, featuring high-kicking girls in long, black silk stockings, was more than five hours long. The producers of this stage piece were the first to use the famous "Banned In Boston" gimmick for promotion of the production. *The Black Crook*'s success depended on audiences pouring into the theater to see what censors and irate clergymen of Boston considered sinful entertainment.

To accomplish their publicity, a minister was goaded into viewing *The Black Crook*, whereupon he immediately wrote a blasting criticism, which was eagerly leaped upon by publicists and widely printed.

The outraged cleric used such expressions as "immodest dress," "short shirts and skirts," "undergarments of thin materials," "flesh-colored tights," "exceptionally short drawers," "tightfitting, extending very little below the hips," "bodice so cut as to show off every inch and outline of the body above the waist," "ladies dancing so as to make their undergarments spring up, exposing the *thing* underneath."

Naturally, a lascivious, large public jammed the theater in order to see for themselves this appalling, awful, gauche, and boorish spectacle.

How can anyone determine the good from the bad except through direct experience?

★ ★ ★

Mack Sennett won everlasting fame as the father of
"The Mack Sennett Bathing Beauty." His short subjects on
the rather scantily attired (for the period) lovelies of the
1910s and 1920s were film fare for an international public.
Goaded by Sennett's creativity, other producers and studios
immediately leaped in and ground out similar films with
"The Cristy Comedy Girls," "The Sunshine Girls," "The
Gotham Girls," and even "The Berkeley Girls."

Sennett first paraded his scantily clad bathing beauties
in 1914 after seeing a copy of the *Los Angeles Times* one
morning with the picture of a very leggy girl on the front
page. She was pointing to a small leg bruise sustained in a
minor traffic accident. On the *Times* page 4, was a one-
column picture and article reporting on President Woodrow
Wilson's impassioned speech concerning the worsening
war situation in Europe.

In a flash, Sennett realized a feminine knee was far more
intriguing than the possibility of the United States
involvement in a war.

★ ★ ★

As in politics, one little slip of the tongue — one action
that would pass unnoticed unless a movie star does it — can
reverberate. Sometimes disastrously.

The incomparable star, Clara Bow, enjoyed — and
rightly so — the international image of the nice girl; the
good, honest, strong-charactered girl. Her fan mail
amounted to thousands of letters per week.

And then, for a time, the tide turned.

Clara went to a Nevada casino, gambled, and lost
$20,000. She wrote a check for her losses, which of course
was accepted because, after all, she *was* Clara Bow. Upon
returning to her studio, the loss of all that money bothered
her so much she consulted with the studio's legal

department. As can happen with legal types, she received some bad advice. It was suggested that she stop payment on the check.

She did just that. The word leaked out to the press, and the headlines immediately blazed:

CLARA BOW IS A WELCHER!

The studio hierarchy was frantic. Clara Bow was the "It" girl — but she had just stopped payment on It! They correctly surmised that millions of dollars of adverse publicity was at stake in the person of the studio's top star.

There were round-the-clock meetings to determine how to save themselves a horror too difficult to imagine. The publicity department came to the rescue, announcing to the press, and on the radio, that Clara Bow's next film was entitiled *No Limit*, a gambling film story. Tons of publicity was ground out of the publicity department's mill, and the world was convinced that what Clara had done was just a stunt.

On the side, the studio settled the debt with the Nevada casino.

★   ★   ★

During the last years of the silent film era, Paramount Pictures had a young comedian named William Austin under contract. He was a big favorite of fans for "lines" he never spoke.

Austin always played the parts of foppish Englishmen, who "spoke" hilarious bits of nonsense in subtitles. (Of course, the actors laughed at these lines, and the suggestion of laughter carried out to the audiences.)

The titles on the screen — the dialogue that Austin was saying in the scene — were written after the filming was completed. George Marion, Jr., then making $2,000 weekly for his titles, wrote many of the words for the silent film stories.

College Humor magazine, one of the most popular magazines of the day (a kind of parent to *Mad* Magazine and *National Lampoon*) ran a joke about a young actress who had been recently signed in New York to go to Hollywood. It was stated that she was scheduled to appear opposite George Marion, Jr., titles!

Sam Katzman, famous oldline prolific producer of 340 money-making low budget pictures, was also a gambler. He favored Scrabble, the letter tile board game. Sam was renowned for betting huge sums on the construction of a word.

One evening when Sam played Scrabble against another known plunger, he wagered several thousands of dollars on one word.

"There is no such word, goddammit!" his opponent hotly denounced.

The die was cast. Sam dived all the way in, insisting that not only was his a bona-fide word, but "I'm using it as the title of my new picture. It's already in the can and about to be released."

The opponent continued to scoff and said he would pay off on the bet only if Sam could prove to him the word was a real one. Sam told the man to meet him at the studio the next day. "Nine-thirty tomorrow morning. I'll show you," Katzman said.

Of course, his vis-a-vis snapped at the opportunity to catch Sam Katzman redhanded.

Sam and his opponent parted. Although it was late evening, he dashed off to the Sunset Boulevard studio, collecting a couple of his top technicians along the way. They worked the remainder of the night setting up the title, filming it, and nursing it through lab processing. Then they edited the title onto the film.

The next morning Sam's Scrabble man showed up promptly at 9:30. Katzman ran the film for him. Sure enough, the title of the piece was the very word Sam had used in the game. The man paid off on the bet.

Sam Katzman and his Scrabble game made possible a new life for a very old word, and it was taken up by the American public consciousness. Its general usage became a part of the *slanguage* and it is listed in several dictionaries.

THE BEATNIK(S), a derivation of *nud*nik. (From *beat* + Yiddish *-nik*: a person having a predilection for unconventional behavior and dress.)

★ ★ ★

Here's a title story for sore eyes.

Hollywood once went through a period where initials were used to identify motion pictures in release. Like GWTW for *Gone With The Wind*; FWTBT denoted *For Whom The Bell Tolls*; and NWMP was *Northwest Mounted Police.*

Linn Unkefer, an RKO publicist, was assigned to handle a new picture starring Jane Russell. He sent out a press release to the newspapers of America, swearing the title of Jane Russell's new picture would never be referred to by its initials.

The film's title?

Tall In The Saddle

★ ★ ★

★ ★ ★

One superstar did not resort to "watergating," i.e., stoutly denying guilt in the face of all evidence to the contrary, but chose to make a public clean breast of his malfeasance in a classic motion picture, *i.e.*, a real turkey.

The movie was *At Long Last Love*, a musical released in 1975, starring Burt Reynolds and Cybill Shepherd. The director was Peter Bogdanovich.

Reviewers seemed unanimous that this was the most shameless, tasteless, infantile, dismal debacle ever to be perpetrated on an already sodden public. Frank Rich called the film "the most perverse movie musical ever made . . . a collossal, overextravagant in-joke. Every time its stars open their mouths or shake their legs they trample on Cole Porter's grave. When the leads break into song and dance at a nightclub or cotillion, the extras just stand there like goo staring off into space; it's like watching a musical unfold within *The Night Of The Living Dead*."

After the umpteenth chorus of miserable reviews and comments, Burt Reynolds, far from demanding a court trial before conviction, sniggered with admirable style. He placed an ad in the trade papers:

I THINK WE BOMBED!

★ ★ ★

★ ★ ★

Hanging some "tag" on a movie star has, many times, helped elevate players to lofty stardom. Clara Bow was named "The It Girl" and Jean Harlow was called "The Platinum Blonde." The incomparable Marlene was termed "Legs" Dietrich, Ann Sheridan was the only "Oomph Girl," and Lana Turner was all "The Sweater Girl" should be, but only Marie McDonald could be classed "The Body."

Tag-hanging has also backfired. Silent screen star, the debonair and dashing Lew Cody, was almost ruined at the box-office when some fool dubbed him "The Butterfly Man."

It caught on with the public!

Poor Lew became a laughing stock, and it took a long time before his popularity was reinstated.

★ ★ ★

In 1922, Cecil B. DeMille filmed his silent screen version of the epic, *The Ten Commandments*. The production was the result of a fine publicity campaign arranged by DeMille's Publicity Director, Barrett C. Kiesling. Already world famous, the renowned director announced he would let the movie public decide what subject he should select for his forthcoming screen epic.

Kiesling made arrangements with the *Los Angeles Times* to make the announcement and to conduct the contest. They would receive the suggestions and ballyhoo the stunt. The prize would be $1,000, a healthy chunk of money in those days.

Eight persons submitted the biblical subject, *The Ten Commandments*, and DeMille declared it the winner, saying he would produce his finest film. At the proclamation of the production DeMille instructed Kiesling to pay the winners $1,000 each.

Giving out the awards Barrett Kiesling interviewed the winners individually, asking them, among other questions, what they would do with the money. And what prompted these persons to suggest this particular Bible story. Some excellent emotional and inspirational copy was gathered, but the response given Kiesling by one winner was never used as it was stated to him.

A 70 year-old jackass gold prospector, single-blanket, gave his reason for wanting to see this motion picture concerning the moral laws received by Moses on the mountain. Kiesling recalled the man's words, and they are here stated, unexpurgated:

"Why? Because, for Christ's sake, I'm a God-damned devout Christian who believes in obeyin ever friggin one of them Commandments. Shit, man, I hope the pitcher will help convince ever sonofabitch in the world who denies God that he's a dumb bastard and a stubborn horse's ass."

★ ★ ★

Kate Smith was the most popular female star on radio in the 1930s. She always opened her show by singing "When the Moon Comes over the Mountain," concluding it by saying, "Hello, Everybody." That cheerful greeting — "Hello, Everybody" — became identified with the great Kate.

Hoping to take advantage of the singer's massive popularity, Paramount Studios signed Kate Smith for one of its early talkies, a musical, which they decided to entitle, *Hello, Everybody.*

Unfortunately, the picture was a flop; it played to near empty theaters all over the country. To make matters worse, newspaper film critics saw a bit of humor in the title. At least 72 of them began their reviews by observing that the film should have been called — *Hello, Anybody.*

★ ★ ★

The "Girl with the Peekaboo Bangs" came by her distinctive title by accident. Very early in her career, Veronica Lake was sitting for some still portraits by John Engstead. She was wearing a dress that had been made for Jean Arthur, whose bosom was somewhat smaller than Veronica's.

At the time, Engstead didn't know Veronica very well, certainly not well enough to tell her that one of her breasts was more exposed than it should be. It was a real dilemma. If he simply ignored the problem and proceeded to photograph her, the portraits would be totally useless.

Then he hit upon a solution. He had a fan on a table just out of camera range, so he walked over and turned it on, directing it at his subject. Immediately the cool breeze on her bare skin made her aware of the problem. She looked down and made the necessary adjustments. As she did so her hair fell over her forehead.

Her hair was still covering one eye when she looked up at the photographer, a mischievous smile on her lips.

Instantly Engstead knew he had to capture that look on film, and he quickly went to work with his camera.

★ ★ ★

Sometimes studios have been able to foresee problems with titles. In the silent era, Paramount bought a story entitled "Nothing Ever Happens," to star Esther Ralston. It was a comedy, but the studio wanted the public to laugh at the picture, not at Paramount. Just before release they changed the title to *Something Always Happens*.

★ ★ ★

★ ★ ★

Metro-Goldwyn-Mayer planned to use the title *Heat* for a motion picture in which the sole star-billing clause was discovered in the actress' contract. Ultimately it was pointed out to the story department and the publicity department and all the executives in the Thalberg Building that such a title could not be used for this particular film's release. Otherwise:

Greta Garbo
in
H E A T

★ ★ ★

When Clark Gable was the King of the MGM lot, Myrna Loy was its undisputed Queen. The studio decided to team them in a picture entitled *Parnell*, which turned out to be so bad that the mere mention of the picture's name would set off laughter and derision.

At the time, MGM also had Rosalind Russell under contract, but she was considered the same "type" as Myrna Loy and was therefore in the Queen's shadow for a number of years. It was no secret in Hollywood that, when Loy turned down a script, MGM assigned Russell to the part. Because her career was in its early stages, she could not afford to turn down a role.

Some years later, Myrna and Rosalind happened to meet at a Hollywood party, and the two were able to reflect amiably on the past. "You know," Rosalind commented, "every script I ever received at MGM had your fingerprints all over it."

"Oh?" Myrna queried with arched eyebrows and a smile. "Where were you when I tried to steer *Parnell* in your direction?"

★ ★ ★

In the early 1930s, the *Los Angeles Examiner* contained a popular Hollywood gossip column written by Erskine Johnson. It was literally one column in width, so its title — "Behind the Make up" — had to be stacked. It appeared as:

BEHIND
THE
MAKE UP

One morning the inevitable happened. The printer made an error on the layout, and the column ran in all editions with the title:

MAKE UP
THE
BEHIND

★ ★ ★

II
DIRECTORS
&
CRAFTSPERSONS

"I have a feeling, Toto, that
we're not in Kansas anymore."

★ ★ ★

In the place that is still termed Hollywood, it isn't only
the actors who give birth to amusing stories and legends.
For instance, the people of the property departments of the
major studios are historically interesting characters. The
demands of their profession call upon them to be highly
creative. One such interesting and creative person of props
was Oscar Lau.

A classic story followed him throughout his long career.
Oscar Lau was assigned to prop the film production of *The
Trail Of The Lonesome Pine* (released by Paramount
Pictures, starring Henry Fonda, Sylvia Sydney, and Fred
MacMurray). Veteran director Henry Hathaway was in
charge of this opus, which was filmed on location in the
foothills of the Sierra Nevada Mountains, in a wooded area
just above the desert town of Mojave, situated some 75 miles
northeast of Los Angeles. At one time Mr. Hathaway had
been a prop man, and those noble worthies swore he
delighted in waiting until the last minute to pose to them
some horrendous problem that had to be solved
immediately, if not sooner.

One day, just before lunch was called, Henry H. lined up
the next shot—a touching graveside sequence presided over
by the film's principals—which had to be photographed
within two hours. Director Hathaway turned to prop man
Oscar Lau and remarked that, of course, they would use
fresh flowers for placing on the grave.

That little goodie had not been in the script, and Oscar
hadn't anticipated it. The desert terrain was notoriously

barren of flowers except in the early spring. It was now autumn.

Nodding assent, Oscar assured the director the flowers would be there.

Dilemma! Panicsville! Oh, Death, where is thy sting!

Oscar walked around in circles for a time, then suddenly bolted for his car. He tore off down the road toward Mojave, leaving a trail of dust and sand in his wake.

Just after lunch, the cast, director, and crew returned to the graveside site to shoot the scene before the cameras. There — his arms bountiful with beautiful, fresh flowers — stood prop man Oscar Lau!

Later, drawn aside and questioned by his amazed co-workers, Oscar told his story. He had remembered that the noon passenger train always stopped at Mojave for about a half hour to take on water for its trek across the desert. He arrived in time to dash into the dining car of the train, thrust a $10 bill at the steward, and pass through the car selecting the nicest flowers from the vases on each of the dining tables.

★ ★ ★

Film star Lee Van Cleef relates a tale that took place during the production of *The Good, The Bad and The Ugly*, an American Civil War story that was filmed in Spain. (Lee's co-stars were Clint Eastwood and Eli Wallach.) A sequence in the story called for the blowing up of a bridge. The special effects and the powder personnel on the project left something to be desired.

The entire bridge had to be blown at once; it could not be a fragmented blowup. On the first try, however, only a quarter section of the bridge went up, on the second try half of the bridge went. While the bridge was again being laboriously rebuilt for retakes, the company busied themselves shooting other scenes. In time they returned to the bridge. This time the very nervous special effects people placed enough explosive charges to blow two bridges.

A portion of the Spanish army was being used in the film, playing both the friendly troops and (changing uniforms) the enemy. The Spanish Commanding General was delighted when he was asked to take the responsibility for pulling the switch to detonate the massive explosion. The General's signal was to be a red flag, which — he was informed — would be waved by a member of the director's staff.

Then it happened!

Someone in the proximity of the director — using a red handkerchief — blew his nose. The General pulled the switch, the entire bridge went aloft with a grand and satisfactory roar. Complete destruction. It was a glorious spectacle.

Not one of the three strategically placed cameras was rolling!

Consternation reigned; there was weeping, wailing, and gnashing of teeth, real and false. The General was undone, miserably abject.

To make amends, the General set his whole army to rebuilding the bridge. Three days later they tried again for the shot. Everything proceeded like clockwork. The cameras rolled the film through the casing; the bridge went up in grand style.

This time the Spanish General was a hero of the American Civil War. In Spain.

★ ★ ★

★ ★ ★

Production managers seldom get credit for the tricks they sometimes have to perform to keep costs down on pictures. One PM was on location for a picture that required considerable action by Indians attacking a cavalry unit. There had to be a great many shots of the Indians racing through a wide river. As they did take after take, many of the Indians were losing their rifles as they fell into the water, and the supply of rifles was running low. To purchase more rifles would strain the budget.

The production man came up with a solution. Each morning thereafter, he would have the rifles attached to the wrists of the Indian extras by thongs, not to be cut loose until the day's work was over.

No more rifles got lost.

★ ★ ★

Almost universally, assistant directors are noted for their ingenuity in handling difficult actors and actresses. Many a subterfuge has been devised by these workers to get stars onto sets and soundstages on time.

One assistant director (probably Chico Day) encountered a problem with three superstar actresses who were appearing together in a film. Each wanted to be the last to leave her portable dressing room and to arrive before the camera when a scene was called. The AD made a pact with them: when everything was ready to go, he would blow a loud whistle, and they could all appear at the same moment.

It worked.

★ ★ ★

★ ★ ★

Director and writer John Huston believed that over-directing his players reduced the spontaneity of their performances. A story is told that one actor, during rehearsal, asked Huston, "Do I sit down when I say this line?"

Huston shrugged. "I don't care. Are you tired?"

★ ★ ★

The well-known makeup artist, Steve Clensos, working on a film project at Paramount Studios, remembers the time when a young and self-appointed expert arrived on the lot, fresh out of the makeup course at Pasadena Playhouse. In the first week, the neophyte desired to prove to all the veterans of the department that he could impress the world with his artistry. He elected to undertake a difficult makeup job on oldtimer, Al Haskins.

Al was agreeable. The young artist worked all morning with painstaking precision, applying the paints and glues, the hanks of hair, using pots and brushes and curling iron, pencils, sponges, and cotton balls. Al Haskins was most patient while he was having the work applied to his personage. Around noontime, the task was complete, and Steve Clensos commented on what a fine job the young man had done. He asked what age Al was supposed to be projecting with this fine makeup job.

The young man replied, with all the confidence of youth, "Oh, I'd say about 65 years of age."

Al Haskins laughed, nearly cracking the expert's makeup job. "Hell," he chortled, "I'm already seventy!"

★ ★ ★

★ ★ ★

Robert "Bobby" Hammack, composer-arranger-pianist, has told a story from the period when he was employed at Universal Pictures.

Within the studio's music recording room hung a huge brass disc, a gong, some 6 feet across, much like the cymbal struck by a muscular, turbaned man that tolled the opening of all of Britain's J. Arthur Rank films.

For years the boys in the orchestra speculated on what deep expression of esoteric Oriental wisdom was contained in the Chinese pictograph stamped upon the center of the polished plate. Finally, the inevitable happened that cleared the mystery for all time.

A group of Chinese businessmen were being conducted on a tour of the studio. When they arrived in the music room and were introduced around, drummer Johnny Williams politely asked the Chinese interpreter if he would please translate the inscription stamped on the gong.

All the musicians crowded close to the interpreter, breathlessly awaiting his words of enlightenment. Putting on his glasses, the interpreter bent close to the brass plate. After a moment he nodded.

"Ah yes," he said sagely, turning to the group. "It says, Chinese Gong."

★ ★ ★

After World War I, General John Pershing made an official visit to the newly merged Metro-Goldwyn-Mayer Studios, with offices on the new Culver City property. William Wellman, then a third assistant director, had been with the famous Lafayette Escadrille and had been decorated by Supreme Commander Pershing in France. He was aware of Pershing's incredible ability to recall the names and faces of all soldiers he had honored.

While the studio big-wigs stood at the entrance to the

studio's cafe waiting for General Pershing's arrival, Wellman stationed himself just inside the main gate. As expected, Pershing saw Wellman and ordered the car to halt. "Hello there, Wellman," Pershing called out. "Come here."

Wellman walked to the car, and the two men shook hands, chatting on and on while the studio brass waited impatiently.

Pershing asked what Wellman was doing, and Wellman explained his position and duties at MGM.

"Is there anything I can do for you?" Pershing finally asked.

"You're doing it right now, sir," the young man replied.

This "chance" meeting caused the company wheels to ask about the identity of the person who had captured the attention of a four-star general. Wellman soon began getting better assignments. A few years later, Wellman directed *Wings*, and the picture was awarded the first Academy Award.

★ ★ ★

We'll set aside the famous (or infamous) Cecil B. DeMille "ready-when" tale. It's so well known it may no longer have Hollywood laughing. Instead we will focus on C. B. and an incident that occurred after the completion of *Northwest Mounted Police*. One of the young stars was Robert Preston (now noted for his great roles in *The Music Man*, *Victor/Victoria*, and the stage production of *The Lion in Winter*).

To drum up audience interest, DeMille took the film company on tour. Acting as master of ceremonies, C.B. was to open the publicity tour at the Paramount Theater in New York. Musing over what he could say about the new, up-and-coming Robert Preston, DeMille's publicity man suggested an idea. Bob Preston was a graduate of the drama and theater arts program of Pasadena Playhouse.

The publicity man told the big director-producer that during Preston's time at Pasadena, he had picked up a portion of his food and rent money parking cars.

Wouldn't it be interesting, the promotion man suggested, if Mr. DeMille had gone to the Playhouse to observe some actor in a role but, instead, had been singularly impressed by the young man who had parked his car for him, one Robert Preston. Then DeMille would have invited him to come to the studio, receive a screen test, be given a contract, and then launched on a film career.

DeMille thought the idea was great. So he told the story from the stage throughout the tour.

NMP and RP were on their way, DeMille style.

Later, when DeMille was preparing and casting another picture, he thought Robert Preston would be excellent for a supporting role. By this time, however, Preston's stock had gone way up, and his career was really on the way. When Bob was approached about doing the new role for DeMille, he read the script, noted he would receive only sixth billing, and turned it down.

C.B. was advised that Preston had declined the offer.

"Why, that ungrateful whippersnapper," DeMille is reported to have said. "If it wasn't for me, he would still be parking cars at Pasadena Playhouse!"

★ ★ ★

D. Ross Lederman, long a director at Columbia, was always known as a very forceful character and an excellent director for rousing action pictures. One day he was called into producer Sidney Buchman's office and assigned to direct the second unit filming of a love scene. It is reported that Buchman went into some detail, carefully explaining how tender and deep the scene was. Every subtle nuance had to be probed and photographed with extreme care and sensitivity.

"Now, Ross," Buchman asked. "How do you feel about this?"

"No problem," Ross exclaimed, slamming his fist into his open palm. "I'll kick the hell out of it."

★ ★ ★

A few years ago there was a chap, Gadabout Gaddis, who appeared in a long-running television sports series, *The Flying Fisherman*. Gadabout himself has told the story that, during the second year of the series, the advertising agency handling the show wanted to make a promotion trailer.

The agency sent Gaddis and a crew, complete with a young New York director, to an Ohio river location for a fishing sequence.

Mr. New York Director knew very little about fishing, but he did know what to do with his camera. At the location he took a long time to explain to Gaddis what the camera's intention was to be. They would start with a long shot from a nearby bridge, then pan over the river and tilt down and pick up Gaddis in the small boat, then zoom in for a close shot. The director said he would use a megaphone to advise Gaddis what was happening so he could be busily engaged preparing the fishing pole, baiting the hook, then casting the line over the waters.

All the action went along as intended. After Gaddis had cast the fishing line into the water, there was a moment of silence.

Shortly, the director's loud voice came through the megaphone. "Now! Catch the fish!" he commanded.

★ ★ ★

★ ★ ★

There is no way to escape the countless anecdotes surrounding Cecil B. DeMille. Nor any wish to do so. DeMille is emblazoned on the heraldic tapestry of film production, of spectacle and promotion — all that was or is Hollywood.

Once, filming a scene for one of his Paramount Studios spectaculars, there were 200 extras on the set, and he was so intent on getting the shot that the company had run well past the lunch hour.

DeMille called for absolute quiet, again explained to all what he was trying to get on film. While he was talking over the public address system, his voice not unlike that of God, one of the female extras spoke quite audibly to the female extra standing next to her.

DeMille singled her out, ordering her to come up on the high platform where he stood. Obediently, she clambered aloft and stood next to him. He remarked that if what she was talking about to her friend was so much more important than what he had to say, perhaps she would share it with the entire company?

Feeling that all was lost anyhow, the girl threw her head back, took a deep breath, and spoke into the microphone. "I said I wonder when the sonofabitch is going to call lunch!"

The crowd was stunned into silence. And so was DeMille. After a moment, he put his hand upon the girl's shoulder, smiled, and called, "L U N C H !"

★ ★ ★

The incomparable director Michael Curtiz was preparing to direct a film at Warner Brothers. Richard Webb was asked to assist Curtiz in screen tests. The director was to choose one of seven nine-year-old boys for a certain role. For the test scene, each boy was to take his position in front of the camera, Webb was to stand next to the camera and (on cue) step in, play the scene with the boy, then return to his position next to the camera.

When all was in readiness, the boy and Webb rehearsed. The sound man said "okay." Mike Curtiz clapped his hands. "Let's go," he said. "Let's go. Everything is silver!"

The assistant director called, "Roll 'em!" The camera operator snapped the camera on and said, "Rolling." A moment later, Mike ordered, "Action!"

When the nine-year-old boy commenced his test, Webb glanced into the little glass window of the film magazine, just at eye level, through which one sees the sprocket that turns as film is fed through the camera. The sprocket, Webb observed, was not turning!

No one else seemed to notice; the operator was looking through the camera aperture; the head cameraman was watching the scene; the sound people continued doing their busy things. When he heard his cue, Webb entered the scene, played it out with the boy, then returned to his position. He looked again into the aperture. The camera definitely was not running.

The scene completed, Mike Curtiz called, "Cut! Print!" Then he beckoned the boy to him. "That was fine," he said to the lad. "Just fine. You tell your mother and father you are a good actor. Who knows, you may get the part."

Going to the cameraman, Webb said, "The damn camera wasn't going."

"That's right," the cameraman replied with a sly smile. "Didn't you hear Mike call, 'Everything is Silver?'"

"Yes, I heard it."

"That means everything works, but nothing works," explained the cameraman. "If Mike doesn't happen to like someone the front office has sent down to test, he won't waste film."

"Everything is Silver" happened with three of the seven boys.

★ ★ ★

★ ★ ★

When director Billy Wilder went to Paris to push
through Jimmy Cagney's starrer, *One, Two, Three*, Billy's
wife asked him to find and ship her a bidet for her
bathroom. Evidently Billy could not locate one for
shipment. He sent his wife a telegram:

UNABLE TO FIND THE ARTICLE YOU WANT
SUGGEST THAT FROM NOW ON YOU STAND
ON YOUR HANDS WHEN YOU TAKE A
SHOWER LOVE BILLY

★ ★ ★

Who says movie audiences don't pay attention? Film
librarian Hazel Marshall had been asked to assemble some
stock footage of large transatlantic ships for use in portions
of a film. The production's film editor, a woman with a high
opinion of herself and of her work, selected from the shots
that Hazel Marshall provided, and had the footage cut into
the film.

First, there was the shot of a huge three-stack ship
leaving English shores. Later a scene dissolved to the same
ship at sea. Somehow it now had only two stacks. When the
ship was shown to arrive in New York, it miraculously
possessed four stacks!

Librarian Hazel pointed out the glaring error to the
editor, only to be archly put down with the statement. "The
audience won't notice; they will be paying attention to the
excellent editing job I have performed."

Prior to the general release of the film, the picture was
seen and reviewed by many critics and columnists. One
very popular Los Angeles columnist, Sidney Skolsky,
caught the two, the three, and the four funneled mistake. He
enjoyed the editor's error and had a ball with it in his

column. Soon the national wire services picked up the mistake and spread the story to all the national press. The goof was exposed to the entire country before the audiences went to see the picture. It could have made the boner of the year award, but it did very well at the box office. People enjoyed going to see the picture to count the smokestacks.

★ ★ ★

Jim Jordan, Jr. (whose father was best known as "Fibber McGee") and Richard Webb produced a movie at Hollywood's Producers' Studio. Lunching one day in the commissary, they were joined by actor Mickey Rooney, also producing and appearing in a film. Their attention was attracted by a comely young lady entering the door. Oddly, she carried her skirt folded over her arm. It was obvious that all she had on below the waist was a diaphanous slip.

The young lady seated herself at a table near their group, nonchalantly draped the skirt over an adjacent chair, and looked casually around the room.

Mickey was intrigued. He smiled at her and said, "Hi."

"Hi," she replied with a nod of the head.

"How come you're not wearing your skirt?" Rooney asked.

"Oh. I have an interview for a part in a picture in just a few minutes."

"Oh, yes, of course," he responded in understanding.

After a silence that seemed quite long, he said to his associates, "she wouldn't want it to get wrinkled, would she?"

★ ★ ★

One springtime some years ago, Sam Wood directed a movie for MGM that had a scene requiring the use of caterpillars. That early in the season the wormlike larvae, which would become butterflies or moths, hadn't yet hatched. No caterpillars could be found. The prop department called some rangers at California's Imperial Valley, where caterpillars were known to show up earlier than other places in the State. The prop men put in their request and were assured the first batch of caterpillars found would be shipped to them.

Meanwhile, to cover themselves, the prop men went to work creating some mechanical caterpillars that could be used by placing a magnet under them to move them around. Alas, the prepared, artful caterpillars did not look lifelike.

The day arrived for filming this particular sequence. Director Wood was understandably annoyed at having to use the phoney larvae but there was nothing he could do about it. The company worked through the morning filming the scenes, having no end of troubles with the mechanical beasties. Right on noon, when the company was about to be dismissed for lunch, the prop man felt a tap on his shoulder by a young apprentice.

"Here's a box of live caterpillars that just came in from Imperial Valley," the young apprentice beamed, shoving a box at him.

This was no time to approach an irate director, who had just spent several frustrating hours of work, informing him it had to be done all over. The prop man hastily shoved the young chap off the set hissing, "Get rid of the goddam things! Get 'em out of here!"

The company broke for lunch.

Leaving the sound stage, no one could avoid seeing a nearby bush alive with dozens of fat, hairy-sleek, multi-colored caterpillars. Director Sam Wood bellowed loudly "What do you mean there are no goddam caterpillars in the United States. Here's a thousand of them on a bush right outside the stage door!"

★ ★ ★

Raoul Walsh was the kind of director who could toss off a line in such a way that — no matter what words or tone was used — offense could never be taken. There might be shock, but it would always be followed by a smile.

When Walsh was directing *Background To Danger* at Warner's (starring Errol Flynn, Alan Hale, Sr., Ronald Reagan, and Allen Jenkins), there was a scene in which a wounded Allen Jenkins was to be brought to a house to be taken care of by the owner's daughter.

The young actress playing the daughter was a relative newcomer, but Raoul was a staunch advocate that if one calls oneself an actor, he or she must be able to act. Professional actors are supposed to know what they are doing.

"Okay! Let's do this," Raoul Walsh called, his usual direction when a scene was ready to shoot.

The young girl approached him. "Mr. Walsh, what do you want me to do in this scene with Mr. Jenkins?"

"Oh," he said offhand. "Play with his balls a little bit."

★ ★ ★

Alfred Hitchcock, as everyone knows, directed the motion picture *Lifeboat*. It was a 20th Century-Fox release, and the fabled Tallulah Bankhead was the star.

Because it was very hot and humid on the *Lifeboat* set, Miss Tallu was accustomed to not wearing her underwear. During most of the film she sat in the bow of a lifeboat, almost always facing the camera. Often she squirmed around, spreading her legs and upsetting the concentration of the crew and the actors who had to work in very close quarters with her.

After quite some time Mr. Hitchcock, in desperation, called his production manager to his side. "You're going to have to speak to Miss Bankhead. Either she will have to put on panties, or she will have to be more careful of the positions she takes."

The PM got out of that one. "No thanks, Mr. Hitchcock, that's not *my* department."

"Well whose department is it?" Hitchcock inquired. "Hairdress? Or Makeup?"

★ ★ ★

Director John Ford, filming *Fort Apache* on location in Monument Valley and using real Indians in the production, consulted with the Indian Medicine Man each morning about what the weather prospects would be for the day. Then Ford would report to the company what the Medicine Man had said. It seemed to work out very well. The Medicine Man was right on with his forecasts.

However, one particular morning, Ford returned from his consultation with the Indian oracle and made no comment to the company. Of course, someone had to approach the director to ask about the weather report.

"He doesn't know yet," director Ford said. "His radio broke down!"

★ ★ ★

A close relationship exists between the stars and director of any film. However, the subtle, potent determination of who is number one is too often present. It can become a tug-of-war, quiet but deadly.

When Josef von Sternberg was the fair-haired director at Paramount Pictures, he had this sort of confrontation with the fair-haired top star Sylvia Sydney. Prior to the filming of the Theodore Dreiser novel, *An American Tragedy*, Teet Carle was given the task of getting together von Sternberg, Sylva Sydney, and co-star Phillips Holmes.

The meeting took place in the portrait gallery, the objective being to compose some photographic artwork of Miss Sydney and Phillips Holmes. Von Sternberg was to lend his artistic talents in posing the two young stars.

Still shots can be singularly uninspired, just one or two beautiful people being photographed in various poses. There isn't much that can be done unless there is an electricity between the parties.

The fireworks began with von Sternberg's addressing Sylvia Sydney as "Miss." "Miss, will you do this," or "Miss, will you look this way." One can hardly blame Sylvia, a distinguished actress, for seething at this definite putdown. She knew it was von Sternberg's cunning way of establishing his authority. Miss Sydney said nothing. Phillips Holmes also remained silent, doing nothing to remedy the situation. However, spectators could see the actress's mind was working.

Then the director changed his tactics. The first time Josef von Sternberg addressed Miss Sydney as "Dear," she did not react. She seemed to pay no attention to him. "He repeated, "Dear, would you please move a little to your right." She still did not respond.

Turning to Teet Carle, von Sternberg asked loudly — and Sylvia Sydney heard it — "What is the young lady's name?"

Teet told the director, "Miss Sylvia Sydney."

"Oh, yes, thank you. Then he addressed the lady. "Miss Sydney," he said. "I was speaking to you."

"Oh, you were?" Sylvia replied. "When you said 'Dear,' I thought you were talking to Mr. Holmes."

★ ★ ★

Michael Curtiz had a favorite prop man whom he employed on every movie he directed for many years. Directing a film at 20th Century-Fox, Curtiz, his trusted properties person at hand, wanted some particular object to use in a scene. He had to have it immediately.

The prop man could not find it anywhere. Michael exploded in high dudgeon. "The next time I need a dumb sonofabitch to do something, I'll do it myself!"

★ ★ ★

It is often recalled that during the 1930s, moviemakers had to submit to the rigid code established by the Motion Picture Producers' Association, commonly referred to as "The Johnson Office." Many a script submitted before production commenced was returned to a studio, heavily blue penciled. In addition, every still photograph taken of a movie star, in or out of a scene, had to undergo the censors scrutiny before it could be released for the advertising campaigns. The Johnson Office imposed a hefty fine for using a still photograph that had been marked "Rejected."

Publicists and advertising people, as well as executives, complained when their campaigns were sabotaged by a blue-nose with a blue pencil. However, there came a day when the whole film industry could laugh at the idiot censors.

Top still photographer, Adolphe L. "Whitey" Schafer, made an 8-by-10 portrait of a shapely girl, with appropriate props, and a male model dressed in a cop's uniform, breaking every one of the Johnson Office still-photo rules.

What were the 10 "Thou Shall Nots?"

1. Law Defeated
2. Inside of Thigh
3. Lace Lingerie
4. Dead Man
5. Narcotics
6. Drinking
7. Exposed Bosom
8. Gambling
9. Pointing Gun
10. Tommy Gun

★ ★ ★

Not generally well known or recognized by the public, but one of the most interesting of people behind the camera was James Wong Howe, director of photography, head cameraman. He was probably the first American-Oriental cinema photographer in Hollywood. (He won several Academy Awards for his brilliant, innovative work.)

Jimmy was born in Portland, Oregon. In his childhood, he had been given a little box camera, with which he became adept. He arrived in Los Angeles in his late teens to try to break into the film business. His first job was with a still photographer named Stagg. Stagg worked freelance for all the major studios. Jimmy Howe started as a delivery boy for the photographer, making his rounds on a bicycle.

The bike bore a sign reading: "Stagg Photos." Jimmy told the story many times that he would be stopped by men asking, "Hey, boy, can I take a look at your stag pictures?"

After awhile, James Wong Howe landed a studio job. Third assistant camera assistant on a Cecil B. DeMille picture. He made so little money that he moonlighted by working his own small photo gallery on the side, specializing in photographing the newer players in Hollywood. His services were attractive because his prices were low.

During those silent days (1912-1913) one of the best known stars at Paramount Studios was Mary Miles Minter. The photographic problem with Miss Minter was her pale blue eyes. In close-ups she appeared to have no pupils. It made her look blind! Her medium shots, long shots, angled shots, could be photographed, but the rule for photographers was to stay away from her eyes.

One day, Mary Miles Minter approached Jimmy to ask if he would be interested in experimenting by taking some photos of her in his little studio.

Indeed he was interested. They made an appointment, and he took the pictures. When the proofs were developed the Minter eyes showed beautifully, sparkling and dark. The actress was thrilled with Howe's results and demanded to know how he had done it. Jimmy didn't know the answer, so back he went to his camera and experimented.

This time he used movie film, doing work over and over, trying to find the secret. What finally occurred to him was that he had used a black velvet scrim, a mesh panel placed outside the camera range to diffuse harsh light.

Mary Miles Minter wielded her power with the studio and demanded that Jimmy Howe set up her lighting and do her photography. In one day, James Wong Howe moved up from third assistant camera assistant to first cameraman. Thanks to his unusual perception and talent he directed the photography for Mary Miles Minter.

And very soon, many, many others.

★ ★ ★

The prolific Western director, George Sherman, filming one of his many pictures in Arizona, used some real Navajo Indians as extras. Their part in the film story called for them to chase — and then be chased by — the U. S. Cavalry.

The men in charge of special effects had driven around behind a mountain some five miles from the camera site to place smoke charges that were to be set off as an Indian smoke signal. This was to be done on a cue from director Sherman. The smoke charges rising in the distance above the mountain would be photographed and edited into the film.

The special effects men signaled by walkie-talkie that they were ready. The scene being photographed was halted, and the camera was turned in the direction of the distant mountain. George Sherman gave the order to set off the smoke charges, and the camera rolled.

After a short wait, the largest mushroom cloud witnessed since Hiroshima arose from behind the peak. The actors and crew of the company stood watching in awe at the unbelievable sight. Out of the silence one of the young, buckskin-clad Navajo actors spoke: "God. I wish I'd said that!"

In the twentieth century, communications still go awry.

There are times, on live television programs, when a breakdown in communication results in disaster. One show, produced in Hollywood for ABC offers a graphic example.

On a particular daytime soap opera, one of those great dramas that reflect all that is good and noble in the American family and the American Way of Life, a director — at the last moment before air-time — redesigned the location of a scene, telling the actors about it and then (in the throes of neglect) failed to inform the camera crew.

On The Air: The cameras were quickly rolled to the set originally planned. There were no actors present. Cut to another set in a far corner of the vast studio. Here the actors stood awaiting the camera so that they could get on with the drama of one American family living their typical American lives — courtships, loves, marriages, deaths, births, murders, mayhems, abortions, conceptions, cancers, corns, comas, rapes, incest, heartbreak, heartburn, headache, and suicide.

Millions of Americans sat before millions of television screens reading three little words:

ONE MOMENT PLEASE

★ ★ ★

★ ★ ★

Film librarian Hazel Marshall offers another candidate for the Goof Award. At the end of one day's shooting on the original *A Farewell To Arms* (Paramount, 1932, starring Gary Cooper, Helen Hayes, and Adolph Menjou, and directed by Frank Borzage), the assistant director compiled his lists of things required for the next day. When he was finished, he turned his lists in to the studio where they were passed along to each of the departments concerned. One sequence for the following night shooting required "100 whorses."

Despite this typographical error, the property department duly filled the request. On the appointed evening, the scenes were filmed at the Paramount ranch in the San Fernando Valley. Cast and crew assembled, the camera was placed, the area lighted and dressed. The script required the World War I retreat of the Italian army, the stragglers — mostly female — following the troops.

Director Borzage called for the "one hundred whores."

The properties man pointed off to the corral. "Over there, sir," he said. "Do you want them all saddled?"

Borzage dismissed the company, asking that someone call casting for 100 Italian-looking ladies for the following day.

The horses were promptly returned to their stables.

★ ★ ★

Director Michael Curtiz always said what he thought to anyone with whom he was working — and always fractured his English. Generally, what he said, left no doubt as to his meaning.

A young actress, who had been assigned to one of his pictures by the front office, over the director's loud objections, was unable to play a certain scene convincingly. Mike built himself into a high fury. During the fifth or sixth *take* of the scene, he stalked across the set, waving his arms at the girl and shouting, "You fock your way into the studio. You fock your way into my picture. Now you are focking up my picture!"

Long after James Wong Howe reached affluence as the film industry's leading cinematographer, he opened a Chinese restaurant on Cahuenga Boulevard out in the San Fernando Valley. In a few months he was reminded that he was supposed to have some publicity photographs taken of himself standing in front of his establishment, to be made into postcards for the restaurant's patrons. Jimmy Howe arranged for a photographer (who was unaware of the background of his subject) to take the pictures. As far as the photographer was concerned, Jimmy Howe was just the proprietor of a Chinese restaurant.

While setting up his camera to take the pictures of the eatery and its owner, the photographer seemed to experience difficulty. He took too much time making decisions on what and how he was going to shoot the pictures, moving about the street attempting one angle and another, while Jimmy stood patiently waiting in front of the restaurant.

Finally, Howe suggested that the photographer might consider using a wide-angle lens on his camera.

The photographer chap drew himself up haughtily. "Look, Mister," he said. "You take care of the fried rice and egg drop soup; I'll take care of the photography."

★ ★ ★

★ ★ ★

William Wyler ranks among the greatest of Hollywood's great directors. He was a brilliant man and a hard taskmaster. However, he could become so intensely involved in the scenes he was directing that he would have difficulty articulating his thoughts to the actors. He knew what he wanted when he saw it, and he would rehearse his cast extensively, frequently reshooting scenes over and over until they were exactly right. The results were invariably good, but getting there could be a strain.

This was often frustrating for the actors in a Wyler picture, but most worked around the problems by discussing scenes with other cast members and deciding themselves how to bring out the internal values of their characters.

Such was the case when Myrna Loy, Fredric March, and Teresa Wright were starring in *The Best Years of Our Lives*, under Wyler's direction. In one scene, however, the stars just could not seem to give the director what he wanted. They rehearsed and rehearsed and rehearsed, and then they took one shot after another, as Wyler became increasingly more agitated — and therefore more incoherent.

After about the fourth take, Wyler's agitation reached a peak. Getting up from his chair excitedly, he rushed up to Fredric March and said something that sounded like, "Glubble-ubble-ubb-dubb." Then he rushed over to Myrna Loy, shook his finger at her in frustration, and said something like "Dibble-ibble-flick-flack." Finally he turned to Teresa Wright, shaking his finger so distraught that no sounds came from his mouth at all.

Returning to his chair, he sat down and managed somehow to gasp, "Let's do it again."

For a moment, the actors stood on the set confounded, having no idea what to do. Fredric March was noted for his kindness and understanding, but this was straining his limits.

With as much restraint as he could muster, he

approached the director and began, "You just came up to me, to Myrna, to Teresa, and you didn't say a goddamned word. You didn't tell any of us . . . . " Then he looked into the director's highly emotional face, hesitated, pondered for a moment. Then he said calmly, "You know, even though you didn't say anything, I think I know what you mean about this scene."

"Yes," Myrna Loy spoke up, "I know what you mean, Mr. Wyler. I don't know how you did it, but you made me understand."

Teresa Wright chimed in, "Yes, Mr. Wyler, that goes for me, too, even though you just shook your finger at me."

They went back to the set, shot the scene, and Wyler was satisfied.

★ ★ ★

The production manager on a picture has many responsibilities. Among other things the PM is concerned with overtime, rentals, wardrobe-fitting penalties, and meal penalties. Often, the PM's job can be quite harrying.

Some years ago, the highly respected production manager Eddie Sieta was working on a Western being filmed at the Iverson Ranch, which is located in the isolated hill country to the northeast of Los Angeles. One day the company was running into overtime, and Eddie — concerned about the budget — knew that every minute was ticking away with dollar signs. He had to get everybody back to the studio as quickly as possible.

Eddie dashed about furiously, getting actors assigned to cars, hurrying the crew into buses, making sure the camera personnel didn't tarry in getting their equipment loaded. Finally he had managed to get everybody on the road back toward town.

It was when he stood waving goodbye to the company, disappearing in a cloud of dust, that he realized he was completely alone — twenty-five miles from the studio with no transportation.

Two Metro-Goldwyn-Mayer properties men tell the story about an incident they were involved in years ago. It happened during the filming of the motion picture *Yellow Jack*, which concerned the yellow fever epidemic during the building of the Panama Canal. The interior photography for the film was accomplished in a heavy jungle setting built on a studio soundstage.

There were several scenes in which mosquitos were to be seen flying into a tent through a slit in the canvas wall, settling then on sleeping soldiers and workers, feasting from them, and thereby infecting them. It was an important story point, because the mosquitos carried the yellow fever.

Photographic tests were made prior to filming the scene, and it was found that mosquitos were so small they didn't show up on the film. Larger mosquitos had to be found and photographed! Immediately!

Naturalists, as advisors to the film company, stated that there was a Culicidae, the "mosquito hawk," a dragonfly, much larger than its cousin the mosquito, but closely resembling it. This larger insect fed on its smaller relative as a staple of diet. The two properties chaps were advised the best time to catch "mosquito hawks" was at night. They could be found in abandoned buildings, like old houses or shacks. One prop man remembered just such a building in Elysian Park, in the eastern section of Los Angeles. It might fill the bill.

Late at night, the two men drove to Elysian Park — fortified, of course, with a few drinks from a handy bottle to keep them warm — and entered the old building carrying flashlights. The anticipation and the fun of locating and capturing "mosquito hawks" provided the men with a greater high than the liquor in hand.

Suddenly, from out of the darkness, a voice commanded them. "Freeze! Raise your hands!"

The following morning the studio's front office received a plaintive phone call from the prop men, who had spent the night in the Los Angeles jail. Would someone please come downtown and bail them out?

Who would believe — least of all, the Los Angeles Police force — that two grown men would really enter an abandoned building in the middle of the night, sucking on a bottle of booze, for the purpose of capturing mosquitos in a glass jar!

★ ★ ★

Some years ago, television director Joseph Agnello worked for Channel 11 in Hollywood. One of his tasks was directing the live series called *Churches of The Golden West.* Joe and his crew — including a Catholic priest acting as Advisor and Narrator — traveled in their mobile unit each Sunday morning to a different church in the Los Angeles area. On arrival at the church location, they would set up their cameras, run the cables from camera positions to the mobile unit, and also hook up a closed-circuit two-way sound system connecting director, crew, assistant director, and the narrator. The assistant director would receive his instructions from Joe, then cue the resident minister when he was on the air, and the worship service would proceed.

The closed-circuit sound was also patched through a public address unit that Joe Agnello could use to talk to the entire crew for instructions prior to air time.

A San Bernardino, California, Protestant church was selected for one particularly warm Sunday morning. The hook-ups were made, everything was ready, and the countdown was on. They were "On The Air." The opening titles were flashed on; the camera outside the church photographed the exterior; the narration by the Priest was recorded; and the scene dissolved to the camera inside the church, where the resident minister awaited his cue to commence.

Watching the monitor in the mobile unit, Joe Agnello spoke to the assistant director over his headset, "Cue the minister."

Joe could see the assistant, but that worthy did not move. "Cue the minister," Joe repeated into his headset.

Nothing. Again: "Cue the minister, AD."

The assistant could not hear him! There was a deathly pause. The minister was standing near the altar with egg on face, looking directly into the camera.

Then the AD spoke into his headset. In the sound system foul-up, his voice came over the public address system, his words reverberating throughout the church, wafting through the open windows into the warm morning sunlight of San Bernardino. "When do I cue the fucking priest?"

The minister, with great presence, commenced talking, and worship began.

Very gently, over Joe's headset, came the dulcet voice of his Reverend Advisor. "Joe, he's not a priest! The line is, 'When do I cue the fucking *minister*.'"

★ ★ ★

III
PRODUCERS
&
EXECUTIVES

"The triumph is all yours,
boss. All I did was follow
your suggestions."

★ ★ ★

When the Legion of Decency pressured Hollywood production companies in the early thirties to adhere to strict rules of decency, the film industry really began donning their "super penetrating glasses."

One example is the RKO film that Lilly Pons appeared in, singing the "Bell Song" from *Lakme* exactly as she had performed it dozens of times on opera stages. She even wore her usual costume.

It was not until the scenes were viewed in a projection room that it hit the studio heads the whole scene would have to be re-shot — or experience the ruthless edicts of the Legion, the film rating arm of the Catholic church.

Miss Pons' navel showed plainly. Horror of horrors!

(For the retakes a narrow strip of fabric was placed across Miss Pons' abdomen.)

★ ★ ★

With *The Jazz Singer*, Warner Brothers launched the era of sound to the motion picture screen. The pictures talked! Al Jolson starred, recording several talking and singing scenes for *The Jazz Singer*. Jolson's fame was on the wane, but his salary requirement was not. To persuade him to take the starring role, Warners offered a modest salary and a percentage of profit from the film. As a result the profit portion made Jolson millions, more money than he would have been paid if he had stuck to his demands. The film's release also renewed his career as a performer.

Paramount's moguls and executives had the same reluctance to meet the demands originally made by Leo McCarey, producer and director of *Going My Way*. But McCarey was determined to make the film with Bing Crosby and Barry Fitzgerald and so he agreed to take no salary for the story, for producing and directing the film.

Rather, he accepted ten percent of the profits. The gamble made McCarey a multi-millionaire.

Indeed, the laugh is on Hollywood!

★ ★ ★

One evening in 1909, a small girl with blonde curls plunked down a dime at the Comedy Theater on New York's 14th Street, Adolph Zukor's first movie house. The theater's manager would not admit the young girl because she didn't look to be sixteen years of age. (At the time, the law would not allow admittance to a movie of anyone under sixteen unless accompanied by an adult.)

The young girl was insistent, telling the manager she was the heroine of the film that was playing. She had never seen the movie. She didn't see it that night either.

The girl was Mary Pickford. Four years later, when she was twenty, Zukor was president of Famous Players and signed Mary to a contract at $500 a week. With subsequent contracts, her salary kept rising until early in 1918, when Zukor lost his star attraction.

Even his offer of a million dollars a year would not keep Mary Pickford.

★ ★ ★

Movie mogul, Samuel Goldwyn, was known for his wonderful ability to gnash and fracture the English language, whether by word or phrase. He was also an

effusive man and was once heard enthusiastically exclaiming to an actress: "You're *terrific*. You're *tremendous*! You're *fabulous*!! You're even *GOOD*!!!"

★ ★ ★

Sam Katzman produced a flock of money-making films for Columbia Pictures and Harry "King" Cohn. Between two volatile personalities, Cohn and Katzman, there were bound to be strained interludes.

During one such period Harry Cohn issued an edict to his executives. "Bar Katzman from the lot! For life!! . . . until we need him again!!!"

★ ★ ★

The tenacity with which some producers and executives pursue a goal is typified in one tittle-tattle tale of the renowned David O. Selznick. When he had produced his smashing success, *Gone With The Wind*, he called his publicity men together and smugly proposed that it would be fitting if a major university would confer on him an honorary doctorate degree.

Of course, the publicists had to agree.

Try as they might, however, no major university could or would be persuaded to favor the request. This lack of inclination and disinterest was reported to Mr. Selznick.

"Well, find two minor universities who will each give me a degree," Selznick is said to have replied. "I'll be satisfied with that."

★ ★ ★

Warner Brothers producer Bryan Foy (The Keeper of The B's), scion of the vaudeville family of "Eddie Foy and the Seven Little Foys," was making a war film, *The Tanks Are Coming*. The film starred Steve Cochran, portraying an Army technical sergeant.

In one scene, the script called for Steve, in full battle dress, chewing tobacco, with fragmentation grenades hanging on his chest, to go into the headquarters building of the General Staff "somewhere in Fortress Europe" to deliver a message. Cochran was to pass an open door of the planning room, stop and eavesdrop on a flock of generals outlining their tactical strategy for stopping the fast approaching German Tank Corps. At the moment, the Germans were attacking the French Maginot Line.

The Sergeant (Cochran) shifted his tobacco cud, barged right in, and told the generals they were all wrong. Then he showed the brass how the action should be conducted. And then, in the story at least, the generals follow the Sergeant's advice!

"Brynie" Foy came in for a good deal of seamy banter at the studio because of this bit of business. He was finally aroused to announce to his detracters: "If I say a technical sergeant told the General Staff what to do, and he wins the whole goddam war single-handed, by God that's what happened!"

He might have added: "And that's box-office!"

★ ★ ★

Before William Thomas expanded his film producing career (Pine-Thomas), he enjoyed himself as publicity and advertising director in Los Angeles for the colorful film exhibitor, Alexander Pantages. Bill tells how, one day, Pantages received a telegram from a comedian who strongly objected to the marquee billing he was receiving for an on-stage appearance accompanying a film playing at the Pantages on Hollywood Boulevard.

Either the billing would be changed or, the telegram stated, "you can count me out."

Pantages immediately fired back a wire to the comedian:

ONE, TWO, THREE, FOUR, FIVE, SIX, SEVEN, EIGHT, NINE, TEN. OUT.

★ ★ ★

It's the smart actor who knows which side of his bread to butter. Especially when he's under stress from the head of the studio.

Actor Grant Withers played a round of golf with Herbert Yates, whose Republic Studios off Ventura Boulevard in what is now called Studio City, had Grant as an up-and-coming contract player.

Yates, on the second tee, flubbed a drive. "Take another, Herb. I distracted you by rattling my clubs," Withers said.

At the third tee, it was a bad hook by Yates. "Take another, boss," Withers said. "That foursome behind us was talking too loudly for you to concentrate."

And so it went, on and on, until there came a drive when nothing happened that Grant could use as an excuse for Yates. Another topped ball. The worst yet.

Wretchedly, Withers sought a last and extreme excuse to permit the boss a second drive. "Swing again, Herb. I was thinking so damned hard it upset you."

★ ★ ★

Singer and actor, Eddie Fisher always wanted to outdo his friend, the flamboyant producer Mike Todd. At the time Todd was married to Elizabeth Taylor.

Mike had a Cadillac limousine, in the back seat of which he had a telephone.

Eddie Fisher bought a limousine, and he installed a telephone in its back seat. Fisher was out cruising and knew Todd was in his car, somewhere. Fisher telephoned him.

When Mike Todd answered his telephone, Eddie said, "Hey Mike. I've got a phone in my car, too."

"Just a minute, Eddie," Mike interrupted. "I've got to take a call on my *other* phone."

★　★　★

When the topper of a British film company visited Hollywood some years ago, he called Warner Brothers Studio to talk with its president, J.L. Warner. The British gentleman was told that Mr. Warner was out-of-town. Asking to speak to the second-in-command, Mr. Solly Biano, the Englishman was informed that Mr. Biano was also out-of-town.

Then he asked to speak with Mr. William Orr, the former actor, who was top executive and Mr. Warner's son-in-law. "I'm sorry, sir," the film man of Britain was informed. "Mr. Orr is all tied up."

The following day the visitor called the studio again, and was told the same thing — of all three executives. On a third attempt, the same news was given to him.

On the fourth day, and upon his last telephone call, Mr. British Film Company was granted the same evasive dialogue.

"It appears," he quipped, "that when Mr. Warner and Mr. Biano go out of town, they always tie up Mr. Orr."

★　★　★

★ ★ ★

Early mogul Hal Roach — responsible for the films of Laurel and Hardy, Harold Lloyd, Charlie Chase, and the Our Gang kiddies — found that pratfalls from banana peels invariably prompted the greatest laughs. In these early comedies, the performers, writers, and directors were always developing newer and greater variations on the old theme.

For Roach, economy was an important factor on his two-reelers. He came up with a way of getting all the banana peels he needed, without having to pay extra for them. The film budget provided lunches for the extras. Usually this was a sandwich and a piece of fruit. Roach ordered that the piece of fruit for his extras must always be a banana.

After lunch, the prop men had the duty of salvaging the banana peels.

★ ★ ★

In the old days, the only thing a person in the film business needed to know was how to get along with the head of the studio. Each mogul, as they were called, was king of his domain. Most of the employees of Warner Brothers held Jack L. Warner to be a tyrant — a master to all, whom all must answer. The correct answer for any situation was probably, "Yes, sir!" And never be flippant. Warner was known to visit movie sets unexpectedly, and no one wanted ever to be caught in any form of idleness.

One afternoon, sure enough, he entered one of his sound stages. Still photographer Clifton Kling was sitting on a canvas-back chair, waiting for the scene being photographed to finish so he could then set up his camera for the still shots.

Warner stormed directly up to Kling. "I notice that every time I come onto this set, you are the only member of the crew who is sitting down. Now, why is that?"

"To tell you the truth, Mr. Warner," Kling replied, "the only time I can find an empty chair is when you come on stage."

★ ★ ★

This is probably the most familiar example of irrepressible studio topper and independent producer Sam Goldwyn's *Goldwynisms*:

"A verbal contract isn't worth the paper it's written on."

★ ★ ★

A special place has long been reserved in film history for the contributions of production executive, Irving Thalberg. The Wunderkind's early death prevented his receiving the designation of "sage" or "pundit," but he did leave behind a few choice pieces of philosophy about the success of succeeding.

"If you are in a position to give credit, do not give it to yourself. You do not need it."

"Never take one man's opinion as final. Never think your own opinion is unassailable."

"Never discuss the many reasons why something can't be done. Remain silent or make positive suggestions."

"The most perceptive man best appraises another man's motives."

"Give your own opinion without reserve; bear no grudge."

NO SMOKING
NO FIRES.

"Do not cater to lower tastes, the lowbrow, vulgar or commonplace. Do not preach."

"Remain incapable of small talk."

★ ★ ★

Nowadays it is the television networks that are the most competitive companies in the entertainment business. It used to be the studios and moguls such as Harry Cohn of Columbia and Jack Warner of Warner Brothers. Then studio heads owned most or all of their own land and stages and made all the decisions. The competition that existed between the "King" and J. L. was fierce.

Where Harry might have received this piece of misinformation will never be known. He telephoned Jack one day. "Jack, it's too bad," Harry said. "I just heard about your backlot burning down."

"Sorry, Harry," Warner replied, always on his guard. "That's tomorrow."

★ ★ ★

Film company executives often make strange decisions. Some editing decisions on a motion picture can frequently come, not from knowing and feeling, but from a chance remark made by a theatergoer.

When MGM sneak-previewed *The Great Ziegfeld*, an overheard remark from a wife to her husband (unsolicited, and therefore considered a genuine reaction) nearly cost Luise Rainer her first Oscar award.

A couple of MGM executives were prowling the lobby after the screening and heard the woman's remark about the film. "Flo Ziegfeld really was an awful heel," she said to her husband. "That scene where he calls up Anna Held

(Luise Rainer) and tells her he has married Billie Burke (Myrna Loy)! He just didn't care that he'd broken Anna's heart. That was cruel!"

The impact of the scene was due to Miss Rainer's hiding her heartbreak to congratulate Ziegfeld (William Powell), not letting her voice betray how deeply she loved him. Her face told all.

The executives were so disturbed by the woman's remark that they recommended the scene be cut before the film was released to the public.

Ultimately, other executives and production personnel voted to retain it. (Probably among them was L. B. Mayer himself, whose criteria for keeping scenes was based on whether he wept or not.) It was the biggest, most important scene Luise Rainer had.

On the strength of it — an unusual number of closeups of her tragic face prevailing — she was voted the Academy Award.

★ ★ ★

This true tale could be titled "The Justice of the Uses of Obscenity According to Harry Cohn." As chief of Columbia Pictures, Harry Cohn has been variously described by those with whom he worked as "base," "high-flown," "high Falstaffian," or any number of other unflattering terms. One of Mr. Cohn's favorite and most savored terms was "son of a bitch." The true meaning of Cohn's utterance of the phrase was determined by the intonation of his voice.

This was brought out quite clearly when director Charles Vidor took "King" Cohn to court, trying to break his studio contract, demanding $78,000 in damages for what he, Vidor, termed "abusive language." A portion of a long Los Angeles newspaper article on the trial (in 1946) points up the suit which shook all the apples in the Hollywood tree.

"Oh, I called him a Hungarian son of a bitch quite

often," Cohn admitted with a shrug. Then, turning to the Judge with palm outstretched in appeal, he added, "But I didn't call him anything bad. We were friends."

Cohn's second in command, B. B. Kahane, testified both Harry Cohn and Charles Vidor used profanity in their many arguments over picture projects. Vidor's favorite, Kahane testified, was "goddammit." But his boss, Kahane defended, was more versatile. Cohn did lean heavily toward using "son of a bitch."

"What did he mean by it," the judge asked.

"Well," said Kahane, "it all depends. When he says, 'Well, *I'm* a son of a bitch,' that means he's surprised. When he says *'That's* a sonofabitch of a scene,' he means it was a perfect scene. When he says 'You're a *son* of a bitch' it depends on *how* he says it."

The judge grew very impatient when Mr. Vidor's lawyers tried to introduce into evidence twenty-three variations of the term "son of a bitch," as used by Harry Cohn. When the testimony was completed, the judge expressed the view that he didn't know why the two parties hadn't consulted psychiatrists instead of coming to court. "I don't know whether this is a lawsuit or a publicity stunt," he added.

The verdict of the court: The court finds that Harry Cohn was accustomed to and in the habit of using obscene language in talking to Mr. Vidor and others. Such language was part of Mr. Cohn's speaking vocabulary. It is used by him as superlative adjectives, not intended by him as insulting or for the purpose of humiliating the plaintiff, and the plaintiff so understood that.

Suit dismissed.

★ ★ ★

Still another lesson in the creative language of Harry Cohn, King of Columbia! It happened in 1946, or thereabouts.

Columbia was preparing a movie, *The Bandit of Sherwood Forest*, starring Cornel Wilde as Robin Hood. The producer worked long and hard with the writers until he felt he had an excellent screenplay. At this point, he sent a copy to Mr. Cohn for approval.

Within 24 hours, the producer was summoned to Harry Cohn's office. "Where the hell did you get the goddamn writers for this script?" Harry fumed and raged. Before the producer could open his mouth, Cohn exploded. "Here you've got something about King Richard . . . hundreds of years ago, in England. And the goddamn knights, too. And the Merry Men are all talking like western cowboys!"

"I don't know what you mean, Mr. Cohn," the producer said, stunned.

Harry slammed the script down on his massive desk, opened it to one of the pages he had marked. "Listen to this shit!" he shouted. "You got these guys sayin' 'Yessiree' and 'Nosiree,' all the way through here." He glared at the producer. "What the hell kind of talk is that?"

The producer looked at the marked lines for a moment. "Mr. Cohn," he said as gently as possible. "The men are addressing the King of England."

"So?" said the Columbia King.

"What they are saying is 'Yes, Sire,' and 'No, Sire.'"

King Cohn struggled for a moment to save face. "Well, it won't play. Change the lines to 'Yes, Your Majesty,' and 'No, Your Majesty.'"

★ ★ ★

Samuel Goldwyn was justly proud of some of the creative people he had working for him, and there were times when he needed to feel a part of the creative process. Choreographer Michael Kidd was one of those creative artists whose work fascinated the great studio boss. Goldwyn was so interested in Kidd's work that he made a pest of himself, popping in to watch Michael work, hanging over his shoulder, and asking questions.

Finally Michael devised a plan that he hoped would so confuse Goldwyn that he would give up his nosiness and leave him alone. One morning, knowing that the studio boss would show up sooner or later, Kidd sat at his desk in his office playing with a dozen black and white cubes, moving them around and grouping them in varying patterns.

As expected, Goldwyn showed up and asked Michael what he was doing.

"I'm working out a dance routine," the choreographer replied.

"Tell me about it," the studio boss said eagerly.

Shuffling the cubes, Michael explained. "These white cubes are positive, and the black ones are negative. I put a black cube here, a white cube here. So what we are getting is negative, positive, then positive-negative. Negative-negative; positive-positive; positive-negative-positive; negative-positive-negative; positive-negative-negative-positive; negative-positive-positive-negative." He went on and on grouping them in ever increasing complexity.

When he was done, Goldwyn looked pensive for a moment, then said, "I like it. Let's do it."

★ ★ ★

★ ★ ★

Frequently, when some notable incident happened to an anonymous studio worker, the publicity department picked up and "assigned" the event to a well-known actor or actress.

The MGM Studio Commissary was famous for its chicken soup. Legend has it that Louis B. Mayer loved this pottage, but as a young man couldn't afford it. When he attained his great seat of power, he saw to it that the studio menu always carried his favorite (with plenty of rice and big chunks of chicken). It cost all of 50¢ a bowl, in the 1930s a high price for soup.

Also at MGM was Jerry Mayer, Louis B.'s brother, functioning in an administrative capacity. On the side, Jerry's hobby was breeding and raising fancy chickens. One day Jerry called a supplier and ordered a rooster and eleven hens, of a rare breed. The cost to him was $50 a chicken, in any decade a lot of money. Jerry Mayer instructed the supplier to deliver the rare chickens to his office at the studio, where on arrival, he would have them transferred to his ranch.

When the supplier showed up at the MGM gate, he told the guard, "I've got some chickens for Mr. Mayer." The guard directed the delivery to the Commissary, where the unusual and rare birds were duly processed — decapitated, plucked, chopped up, and boiled — to appear in the noon soup.

On discovery of the grave error, the publicity department reasoned, why attribute such a good tidbit to Jerry Mayer?

So, the story was released as having happened to the up-and-coming contract actor, Robert Young (who would later be everyone's dream of an American father). Instead of being appreciative at receiving national publicity, Young was upset. A couple of his relatives had been dunning him for loans, which Young — on a small salary — could not afford.

On the day the chicken-soup story broke, he received phone calls from several of these relatives. How was it, they wanted to know, that he could not loan them money, when he could throw away six hundred dollars on a flock of chickens!

Harry Cohn's brother Jack was the financial wizard in the Cohn family, but occasionally Jack tried to express his views on artistic matters. On one such occasion, Jack approached Harry with the suggestion that Columbia ought to get onto the bandwagon of Biblical epics. "The other studios are coining dough with them," Jack is reported to have argued. "Look at the success of DeMille. The Bible is full of stories ripe to be taken, and you don't have to pay any author's royalties."

Resenting his brother's efforts to get into matters he knew nothing about, Harry challenged Jack. "You have no idea what you're talking about," he said testily. "You're no expert on what kind of stories there are in the Bible. You don't know anything about the Bible at all. I'll bet you fifty bucks you don't even know the Lord's Prayer."

Jack took the bet. Each brother put up their fifty dollars in cash, and Harry prodded Jack, "Go ahead."

Jack recited, "Now I lay me down to sleep. I pray the Lord my soul to keep. If I should die before I wake, I pray the Lord my soul to take."

Harry heaved a sigh and shoved the money toward his brother. "I guess I lose," he said. "I never would have believed you knew it."

★ ★ ★

★ ★ ★

Few people ever got the best of Harry Cohn. However, on one occasion, the actress Rosalind Russell managed to come out even in a confrontation with the King of Columbia. She had made several successful pictures for the studio during the early 1940s. After one of these, she was scheduled to entertain the U.S. troops. The delightful Miss Russell was a charitable lady, but she was also a good businesswoman.

She needed a wardrobe for the tour, and the Irene costumes she had worn in her last picture were perfect. Since she was doing her bit for the war effort, she expected Harry Cohn to do his. She went to the studio head to ask for the favor.

Harry Cohn declined, explaining that he could not afford to loan or give away costumes because of war shortages in materials. "However," he added shrewdly, "we could sell them to you at cost."

Rosalind was outraged by Cohn's response, but she maintained the dignity and grace for which she was noted. "How much?" she asked.

After making a phone call to the accounting department, Cohn informed her, "$3,300."

"I'll take them," the star replied, "if they can be delivered to your office right now." After Cohn accepted the terms, Rosalind wrote out a personal check and gave it to him. All this time, her anger was working silently inside for a way of expression.

It was after the wardrobe had been delivered and she was preparing to leave Cohn's office that the idea occurred to her. She turned to the studio head and said, "By the way, there is one other matter I need to settle with you. Because of the war shortage, the wardrobe department was unable to find a suitable fur coat for the picture, so we had to use mine. I understand the studio usually pays $100 a day to rent furs of this quality."

Cohn admitted that this was customary. "How many days was it used?" he asked.

"Twenty-seven days," she informed him. "But you may want to check with the production manager to be sure."

Cohn checked, then wrote out a check to Rosalind for $2,700.

The star was able to leave the studio with her wardrobe, check, and satisfaction.

★ ★ ★

Before moving to Hollywood, producer and director Larry Buchanan was based in Dallas, Texas. From character actor Chill Wills he received an invitation to visit the set of *The Alamo*, filming in Bracketville, Texas. The film was destined to garner several award nominations including a Best Supporting Actor nomination for Wills. *The Alamo* was one of the first motion pictures to employ the new, huge 65mm camera, called the BFC. (The 35mm camera, heretofore the standard camera, was called BNC.)

Not familiar with the BFC, which had to be hoisted around by a crane, Larry Buchanan innocently asked what the initials stood for?

The head cameraman looked at the camera and then turned to Larry. "Big Fucking Camera," he said.

★ ★ ★

IV
ACTRESSES
&
ACTORS

*PLEASE DON'T FEED
THE ACTORS*
— A large, hand-lettered sign
hanging on wall of Stage 5,
Paramount Studios, c. 1940.

★ ★ ★

One lovely young starlet — unidentified by name to protect her innocence — showed great promise as a film actress, and was signed to a contract at Paramount in the late 1940s.

Before long it was noted and commented upon that she was always seen about the lot carrying a Bible under her arm.

Talent executive Bill Meiklejohn was curious and one day asked her why she carried it.

"In my religion," the starlet responded, "we carry the Holy Bible wherever the Devil is present!"

(It was quite some time before she could be persuaded to tote her Devil Chaser inside her shoulder bag.)

★ ★ ★

Greta Garbo was not really the naive Swedish girl many considered her to be. Among her capabilities was that of coping with a bluff from studio executives. Once, when her contract was being renegotiated at Metro-Goldwyn-Mayer, the brass in the front office were determined to frighten her into giving up some of her demands.

The last picture on the existing pact was about to start production. Garbo was notified that Aileen Pringle would assume the starring role and Garbo, to fulfill her contractual obligation, would portray a maid.

Miss Garbo responded calmly to this news, not protesting to the front office. When studio executives learned she had arranged to be fitted for a maid's costume, they arranged to give in to her demands. A star is a star is a star.

★ ★ ★

Joan Blondell was the star of many Warner Brothers musicals. She once told columnist Hedda Hopper about an unusual experience she had in Las Vegas.

One evening before she was scheduled to return to Hollywood, she decided to wander through a casino to watch the activities. Miss Blondell was a non-gambler and knew nothing about gaming. However, a dealer at one table urged her to try her luck. So she purchased $20 worth of chips and followed the dealer's instructions and suggestions on how to bet on a roll of the dice.

In time she won $750. "Why don't you quit and cash in your chips?" the dealer suggested.

She decided to accept the advice, handing the dealer the dice.

"That pays for the baby," he commented.

She had no idea what the dealer meant by the remark, and it bothered her for a week. Then she remembered. A few years earlier, she had talked a young un-wed actress out of having an abortion. "I'll finance the birth," Miss Blondell offered.

The young girl left Hollywood with the baby. Later, Joan learned that she had met and married a man in Las Vegas. She had told her new husband the story of her baby.

The total financing of the birth had amounted to $750.

★ ★ ★

Allison Skipworth was famous for playing frowsy, bewildered, elderly women. She was a contract player at Paramount when Mae West appeared in her first Hollywood picture, *Night After Night*.

Miss Skipworth deduced that Miss West was a fresh face who might easily steal every scene of the picture. That irked Miss Skipworth.

Desperately needing to establish herself as a power, Miss Skipworth said to Mae, "I'd like you to know I am an actress."

"Don't worry," Mae West replied from the corner of her mouth. "I'll keep your secret for you."

It would require volumes to record all the witticisms and quips of W. C. Fields. Off camera, Fields was a member of an elite and frolicsome coterie that included such luminous aristocrats as John Barrymore, Gene Fowler, John Beck, artist John Decker, and Errol Flynn. The clan assembled frequently at Decker's digs in Beverly Hills, just for conviviality.

Included in this august clique — when he would sally forth from his hogan on the Morongo Indian reservation near Banning, California — was an unbelievable caricature of man named Sadakichi Hartman, who was half-German, half Japanese, and almost totally mad. He was a practicing ne'er-do-well — poet/essayist/ballet dancer/art critic/author, or such were his claims.

W. C. Fields could not abide the dirty, unkempt, crumply attired Sadakichi, and his disdain did not go unnoticed by Hartman, who retaliated by flaying the comedian with a rapier tongue.

Once, after Sadakichi had punctured W. C., the twangy comedian recoiled, drew himself up to whatever height he could muster, and assumed a hurt, innocent countenance.

"Why do you hate me?" Fields plaintively complained. "*I never tried to help you?*"

★ ★ ★

It didn't take Lupe Velez long to create fodder for the gossip mills of Hollywood. She acted instinctively, on and off the set, and received a lot of attention and publicity. One of her first acting breaks was opposite Douglas Fairbanks.

One day on location, a horse bit her on the arm. The gutsy Lupe did not jump away, nor did she yelp and scream. She merely turned to the horse and bit him on the neck.

The horse backed off.

★ ★ ★

Reading that Paulette Goddard had auctioned for more than three million dollars the art collection she and her late husband, Erich Maria Remarque, had assembled over many years, MacDonald Carey recalled that the glamorous Paulette was always an astute business woman. Miss Goddard was seldom content unless she received dollar value for her contributions to show business, whatever they might be.

"One of the several movies I made with Paulette was *Hazard*," Mr. Carey had said. "She played a wealthy woman, a compulsive gambler chasing around the country pursuing Lady Luck at the gaming tables. I was a detective hired to find her and get her back to her home. When the director did not like the four pieces of luggage the prop department chose for her, Miss Goddard suggested she had a set that would be perfect."

And it was perfect.

As actress, she was paid a huge salary. For the use of the luggage, she was delighted to accept a check each Saturday from the properties man for $20.00.

★ ★ ★

Some Hollywood stories are merely legend. Others really did happen. One true tale pertains to the lovely and exciting Kay Francis. Will anyone forget *One Way Passage* or *Trouble in Paradise*? At the time of this particular event she was married to actor and writer Kenneth McKenna. The couple were at home one evening, and Kay answered a loud knock at the front door. "Miss Francis?" asked the attractive, distinguished European man.

"Yes," she replied. Thinking he must be someone she had met or someone her husband knew, she invited the gentleman in. They went into the front room, and the three sat and chatted idly for some time.

"This is all very intereting," the distinguished man said finally. "But as you know talk isn't what I came for."

Kay inquired what he meant by the statement.

"When are you going to let me choose one of your girls?"

"What girls?" Kay asked.

"Isn't this the home of Miss Francis? Miss Lee Francis?"

It was at that moment that Kay Francis and Kenneth McKenna learned that for six months they had been living next door to Lee Francis, the number one Madam in Hollywood.

★ ★ ★

Muriel Angelus was a musical stage sensation in England. In the early 1940s she became a classic Hollywood beauty under contract to Paramount Pictures. Typical of the whys or wherefores of film executives, she never was allowed to use her beautiful singing voice in films.

The famous composer Richard Rodgers was a close friend of Muriel and her husband Paul Lavalle, the orchestra conductor. He implored Muriel to audition for his musical production, *The Sound of Music*. Rodgers and lyricist-collaborator Oscar Hammerstein needed a singer for the Mother Superior role. Miss Angelus agreed to audition.

After hearing her sing some of their music, Mr. Rodgers approached the artist. "Muriel, you sound too young," he said. "Could you perhaps sing a little older?"

★ ★ ★

Veteran radio, television and motion picture actor, Cliff Arquette, the lovable "Charlie Weaver," was doing a part in a picture when he was in his sixties. Appearing with him was a virile, handsome, and highly obnoxious actor-stud. Each morning and throughout each day of production, the stud regaled Cliff with his sexual exploits, giving every detail of conquest and seduction.

One day the actor was rhapsodizing about his no-less-than three scores of the previous night. Cliff was finally fed up. "You can't possibly have been to bed with all the girls you've been telling me about," he said.

The stud hotly demanded to know why not?

"If you had bedded all those girls in such a short time, you'd look like me!"

★ ★ ★

If anyone has doubts about how gimmicks can gain the attention of the important folks of Hollywood, just ask Victor Mature.

When he was trying to break into pictures, Victor cooked up an idea that worked. He erected a tent on a vacant lot across the street from the offices of Cecil B. DeMille, himself a master of promotion. Victor swore he would stay in the tent until C. B. granted him an audition.

Mature's best friend, Carl Schroeder, the magazine writer, did his best to talk Vic out of this bizarre residence, insisting the idea was too corny to work.

Victor proved him wrong. One day, DeMille came out and talked to the little-known actor for some minutes. Later, Mature was DeMille's choice for Samson to Hedy Lamarr's Delilah.

★ ★ ★

W. C. Fields' longtime friend was star Warner Baxter. One day in 1944, they walked and talked together along Hollywood Boulevard.

Approaching them was the rising young star, Gregory Peck. Fields turned to Baxter, clutched his arm, and spoke in an urgent, twangy voice. "That man coming toward us. I've met him at least a half-dozen times. I have a terrible time remembering names."

"That is young Gregory Peck," Warner told Fields.

"Gregory, how nice to see you," Fields said when the three met a moment later. "How are you?" Fields turned to his longtime buddy then. "Gregory, I want you to . . . uh . . . ah . . . to meet . . . uh . . . my old friend . . . Oh Shit!"

★ ★ ★

At the height of his career, Roy Rogers demanded more money from Herbert Yates, head of Republic Studios. When Yates argued that Rogers was just another cowboy star, the actor protested. He wasn't just another cowboy; he was the number one in Westerns, recognizeable by every kid in America and most of their parents.

Yates was not convinced. "Without the white cowboy outfit and the big hat," he said, "you would be just a singer named Leonard Slye."

Roy took this as a challenge and decided to parade down Hollywood Boulevard in civvies, to prove to Yates he would be mobbed.

To Roy's chagrin, he attracted no notice. Then Roy saw a smiling face approaching, and he was relieved. At last he had been recognized. When the man reached the star, he thrust out his hand, exclaiming, "My God, Lenny Slye, where on earth have you been? I haven't seen you in years."

★ ★ ★

The late Sam Jaffe and Zero Mostel were an unlikely pair of close friends. It was a case of the gentle and soft-spoken in harmony with the ribald and loud. "We both saw the world at a tilt," Jaffe explained.

Once Margo and Eddie Albert gave a black-tie dinner party in honor of Laurence Olivier, and the great British actor requested that Jaffe, whom he had not met, be invited. Margo feared that Olivier might not relate well to Mostel, so she asked Jaffe not to tell his boisterous friend about the party.

But Jaffe had a sense of humor, unsuspected by the Alberts. He did more than tell Mostel about the event.

As the guests were dining, Zero Mostel entered, his rotundity garbed as a waiter. Taking a place at Olivier's elbow, Zero suddenly scolded loudly, "Sir Jocko, for shame! You're using the wrong fork!"

Sir Larry proved to have a sense of humor, and the party broke up in successful bedlam.

★ ★ ★

There are numerous Hollywood anecdotes, myths, and legends that explore the stumbling blocks and stepping stones of career advancement. Some talented persons are their own stumbling blocks. Others know a stepping stone when they see it.

Clara Bow learned some facts about reporters the hard way. The lovely Clara may not have comprehended that she could do nothing without notice. Chalk it up to being from Brooklyn.

She was uninhibited, and she often became involved with men who could create uncomfortable situations. One such was a handsome young dentist of Beverly Hills, who had a wife. When the wife found out about their affair, she was vindictive, to put it mildly. The lady filed for divorce and went off to her former hometown, Dallas, threatening to sue Clara for alienation.

The situation worsened, and Clara chose to settle the matter herself, without help from lawyers or studio executives. She got on a plane and flew to Dallas to meet the wife and pay her off.

Miss Bow's arrival in Dallas did not go unnoticed. One woman of the local press guessed why she was in town, and called Clara's hotel room. "Is it true," the reporter asked, "that you are here to pay Mrs. 'X' $50,000 to call off a lawsuit against you?"

"Is that what she's telling?" Clara flared back angrily. "She promised to settle the whole thing for $25,000. And that's all I'm going to pay her."

Now, take a bow, Fay Bainter!

Miss Bainter, whose illustrious stage and screen career spanned several decades, always smiled knowingly and tolerantly when she overheard an actor or actress complain about a role being "too small."

A "too small" role brought Fay her greatest fame — as Ming Toy in *East Is West*. (She related this story about 40 years ago, when she was filming MGM's *Young Tom Edison*, playing the inventor's mother.) "The (Ming Toy) role was the shortest of any character in the play," she said. "When I read the script (sent to her by producer William Harris, for whom she was under contract for stage roles), I was shocked at how few 'sides' the Ming Toy part afforded."

Miss Bainter had played several Shakespearean roles and had completed a two-year run in George M. Cohan's *The Willow Tree*, a play in blank verse. "I shrank from doing a character who was little more than a different kind of Cinderella," she said. "I had not yet learned that Cinderella will never be a flop with the public."

Miss Bainter, skimming through the script, failed to note that much of the dialogue of the other characters in the play was devoted to the unseen Ming Toy, with each scene building to her appearance. "I turned down the role, but then I was reminded that I had a contract with William Harris and I must fulfill it," she said.

"I really expected the play to close in a week or two. But it ran for five years!"

★ ★ ★

Carole Lombard was a star with beauty and brains. Before she met and married Clark Gable, Carole had been signed to a term contract with Paramount Pictures at a salary of $3,000 per week, payable 40 weeks of the year.

During her first two contract years, the studio put her into every picture they possibly could. At the end of the second year, she was called into the front office and told that she was not developing into the big star they'd hoped. She could either sit out the remaining year of her contract, collecting her $3,000 a week, or take the money in a lump sum and leave the studio immediately. Carole announced that she would sit it out.

Then she wasted no time. Each day she called Paramount to inform them where she could be reached. She enrolled in a flock of courses — voice, dancing, cinematography, acting, screen writing, motion picture production, directing. The entire nine months was spent in learning the technical arts of the screen business. When she left Paramount, there was little doubt she was the most knowledgeable actress in the film business.

A year later, when she had completed a film for David O. Selznick, she arranged for a large press conference. At the time, income taxes were taking a bigger and bigger bite, and there was a lot of grousing, especially among the top-salaried stars. To the press, Carole announced her great pride in being an American — proud to receive $200,000 for a picture, proud to be able to repay her government with the taxes upon the huge sums she received. The public had made her a star, and rich. She played the press conference straight and garnered tons of publicity.

Just Carole's subtle way of informing Paramount Pictures to take their measly $3,000 a week for 40 weeks that they had "thrown away."

★ ★ ★

Clara Bow was not all stumbling blocks; she could be a stepping stone, too. The "It Girl" was known to help newcomers in their attempts at screen careers.

Once Clara approached Teet Carle, her friend and confidant at Paramount, pointing out to him a cute blonde girl. "She's new," Clara said. "She can use some publicity. See if you can help her."

Teet introduced himself to young Harjean Carpentier. He arranged for a still photographer to make some head shots of the young starlet.

Alas, nothing seemed to come of the attempt at the time. The young girl changed her name, and a few short years later she clicked, becoming MGM's hot property — perhaps the hottest property in town. Clara Bow's introduction to Teet Carle and his introduction to the still photographer did help Harjean Carpentier along the way to becoming Jean Harlow!

★ ★ ★

★ ★ ★

Deborah Kerr's last name, pronounced "Car," is confusing to many people, who pronounce it "Cur" until corrected. One evening after attending a studio premiere, she came out of the theater, where the limousines were lining up to collect their passengers. The announcement came over the loudspeaker: "Miss Cur's car . . . er . . . Miss Car's cur . . . Oh . . . Miss Car's car."

★ ★ ★

Like many other beautiful starlets signed by major studios in their heyday, Susan Hayward came to Hollywood with dreams of big stardom. Eventually her dream came true and she became one of the great screen actresses of the golden age of films, but for many months she saw only the lens of still — not movie — cameras as a Paramount "contract player." Susan's shapely figure was posed in bathing suits and short-shorts week after week for publicity photos. They showed her cavorting on the beach and stagily celebrating all sorts of holidays — official and unofficial. These pictures saw print in newspapers and film magazines all over the world.

She continually asked, "When do I get a part in a movie?" Always she was told by the talent department, "Be patient. You're being groomed for the future."

When it came time for the Paramount national sales convention in Los Angeles in 1938, Susan was ordered to show up at the hotel ballroom, where sales people and exhibitors were gathered. She was one of many stars and starlets appearing before them to ballyhoo Paramount pictures.

Susan was announced, and she walked onto the stage to loud cheers from the assembly. Taking command of the microphone, she spoke to the group. "I notice you

—88—

recognized me," she said. "How many of you have seen me in still pictures?"

A flood of hands were raised.

"Has anybody seen me in a movie?" she asked.

There were no hands, only laughter.

"How many of you would like to see me in a picture?" she asked.

The response was a huge roar of applause.

"Then would you tell the studio about it?" she asked. "They won't listen to me."

She soon got cast in her first picture, quickly becoming a big star, and eventually winning the Academy Award for her role in *I Want to Live*.

★ ★ ★

Addison Richards is still regarded highly. His versatility as a performer shows in 200 Hollywood films. In the early 1950s, Richards was called to New York for a leading role in one of the shows of the television series, *Lights Out*.

The director of the show in which Richards was cast was just out of college workshops, very intense, and unaccustomed to working with professional actors. He had the unnerving, sophomoric habit of probing the actors during rehearsal, beseeching them to tell him: "What are you thinking? What do you have in mind?"

When the time came for Addison to rehearse a portion of his role in the suspense-mystery story, the director instructed him to concentrate on his interpretation of the character. "Just what do you have in mind at this point?" the young man asked in a serious tone.

Oldtimer Addison thought about the question, paced the rehearsal room for a few moments. "What is your idea, your motivation for the role, Mr. Richards?" the director prodded.

"Money!" Richards replied pointedly.

★ ★ ★

When a film star has the power and status to make things happen, it is often for the good of society. Sometimes it — the use of fame — is done in a large way, and it is recognized and commented upon by the entire population. Sometimes it is no more than an expression of a humanity recognized by only a few.

An example of the latter is the legendary star and wonderful person, Barbara Stanwyck.

To close associates, she is "Missy." One production manager has shared with only a few persons a story about Barbara Stanwyck during a motion picture made on location. The setting was a southern city where, at the time, the color line was decidedly and rigidly drawn.

Prior to the company's departure for this particular American city, the production manager informed Barbara that she and the cast would be put up at the plushest hotel in town. However Miss Stanwyck would not be able to have the two-room suite she had requested; one room for herself, and one for her maid, Harriet Coray. The hotel's management would not accept a black person as a guest. There was a very fine hotel for black persons across town that, the PM was informed, would comfortably accommodate Harriet.

"Forget the plush hotel for me," Miss Stanwyck said to the production manager. "If I'm going to need Harriet, I'll need her all the time. Make a reservation for me at the same hotel where Harriet will be staying. I don't believe *they* will refuse *me* a room!"

★ ★ ★

It has been said that Chinese star Anna May Wong had total recall. She possessed the uncanny ability to remember places, people, and events or information after many years.

Dutch Ergenbright was once introduced to Anna May Wong. "I know Mr. Ergenbright, the magazine writer," she said.

Dutch demurred saying she was mistaken; they had never met before that moment.

Miss Wong proceeded to tell Ergenbright at what party they had met, the date of the party fifteen years earlier, the name of the girl he had escorted and a string of incidents that had occurred at the party.

This left no doubt in Dutch Ergenbright's mind that Anna May Wong, the mysterious Chinese actress in Hollywood, was mysteriously miraculous!

★ ★ ★

Claudette Colbert, for some years now a resident of the Island of Barbados, was a product of the Broadway stage. She arrived in Hollywood in the early days of talking pictures. A dramatic actress of conviction, she stated publicly that she would never resort to the standard starlet ploy of being photographed in a bathing suit. She didn't need it; such displays were for those who depended on things other than talent and for Sennett's Bathing Beauties.

After her career had been firmly established one young photographer at Paramount, John Engstead, was assigned to photographing Miss Colbert at her home, around her pool. Despite her firm rule, he tried to persuade her to pose in a swimsuit.

Claudette answered his requests politely, saying she was an actress who did not put her anatomy on display.

He pointed out that she had shown her long legs as Poppea, in *Sign Of The Cross*.

She countered with "I had to do that to properly play the role of a wicked queen."

"Then how about hoisting your skirt as you did in *It Happened One Night*?"

"That," Miss Colbert informed Mr. Engstead. "That was a story point."

"So," he said. "It's all logic!"

She nodded agreeably.

"You have a pool that has been photographed many times," the photographer said. "It's obvious *you* swim in it."

Miss Colbert admitted that she did.

"So," said John. "What do you wear while swimming? A Mother Hubbard?"

With no rebuttal at hand, Claudette posed in a swimsuit — and often did so in subsequent years.

★ ★ ★

Lucille Ball opened her front door one day, responding to the ring of the doorbell. She confronted three Japanese tourists, wearing severe dark suits, with cameras hanging around their necks.

The three men bowed respectfully toward Miss Ball, who, being *Lucy*, was inclined to bow back. She did tilt her head just a little.

Two of the dark-suited visitors looked expectantly to the third dark-suited companion, deferring to him to convey their collective message.

"We ruv Rucy," the man said.

Then the three men, with triumphant smiles on their faces, slowly backed away, bowing.

For some, happiness is still a television re-run of *I Love Lucy* someplace on the planet.

★ ★ ★

To promote a rapidly rising young comedian he was pleased to represent, publicist Bert Ford dreamed up a fraternal organization called *The National Order of Jesters*. To get promotion space for his young comedian, Bert announced to the trades (*Daily Variety* and *The Hollywood Reporter*) that his client had just been awarded the NOOJ kudo, "Jester of the Year."

On the day the press release appeared in the trades, Bert and his client were making the rounds of the production offices at 20th-Century-Fox Studios. In one of the corridors of the administration building, they encountered an over-the-hill comic.

The old comic extended his hand to the young comedian. "Congratulations on getting the Jesters' Award, ole buddy," he said. "Believe me, it's big stuff. I know. At my peak I was given the award two years in a row!"

★ ★ ★

One day, John Barrymore stopped off at *Lucey's*, his favorite watering place, not far from Paramount and RKO Studios. After having a convivial drink (or four or six, etc.) with some of his cronies, there came a time when he had to relieve himself. He made tracks to the Men's Room.

Perhaps it was the low-key lighting, or his blurred vision, or the pressures of the bladder that caused him to blunder into the Ladies' Room. In any event, while he was finding relief in a toilet, a woman entered.

"How dare you!" she exploded in a shocked voice. "This is for ladies!"

Barrymore turned to the woman, his relief valve in hand, and bowed gallantly. "So, madam, is this!"

★ ★ ★

★ ★ ★

Star Robert Mitchum, appearing in the production *Anzio*, being filmed on location in Europe, was on a beach one day. A young lady rushed up to Bob, shucked her blouse, and stood in front of him, bare-breasted.

The unflappable Bob looked her over for a moment and nodded approvingly. "Very nice," Mitchum said. "What do you do for an encore?"

★ ★ ★

The matchless Sherlock Holmes (sorry, have that read, "Basil Rathbone") was back east in New York performing in a play. During one scene in which five actors were onstage, there was a moment of silence where there should not have been silence. A line had been dropped.

Offstage, the prompter hissed out the line. But the silence continued.

The prompter moved closer, almost onto the stage, close enough that part of the audience could see him. In a loud whisper, he threw out the line again.

Rathbone, without moving a muscle, spoke out in a normal voice. "We know the line, old boy. But who says it?"

★ ★ ★

MacDonald Carey, the popular motion picture leading man, now starring in the television series *Days Of Our Lives*, recalls an anecdote from his early days at Paramount. It was 1942 when his star began to rise, after joining Rosalind Russell and Fred MacMurray in the movie, *Take A Letter Darling*.

On the night when the film was previewed, the studio

had comment cards distributed to the audience as they entered the theater. The cards requested the audience jot down their reactions to the actors, and also to the story. Mr. Carey grabbed the most attention and comment, the audience being unanimous in wanting to see more of this "interesting, exciting young man."

The following morning, the Paramount production chief, Henry Ginsberg, called MacDonald to his office — "just to chat." Mr. Ginsberg did most of the directed chatter. "I suppose you've already seen the preview cards, Mac?" he asked.

"Yes, I've been going through them," Carey responded.

"Well, we don't want this kind of thing to go to your head," Ginsberg said. "The audiences pay their money to see Rosalind Russell and Fred MacMurray. You don't bring any money into the box office."

"I understand that."

"Just because you've got good comments on the cards, we hope you won't get carried away and begin asking for more money."

"I won't," Mac smiled. "But, my agent will!"

★ ★ ★

He of the Velvet Tones, Mel Torme, tells one on himself. He has been credited with discovering the unequaled impressionist, Rich Little. As Little moved onward to gather fame, he and Mel Torme worked together a good many times. Both claim to like one another very much.

Rich Little has publicly acknowledged Mel's sponsorship during his early days. Not too many years ago, they both played their acts at the Sands Hotel in Las Vegas. The billing on the marquee outside the hotel read "RICH LITTLE" and beneath that, "MEL TORME."

A very old friend of Mel's, who had for many years been living in Switzerland, returned to the United States to visit. Mel invited him to his show at the Sands. When Mel and pal approached the hotel, Mel noted a strange expression pass over his friend's face. "What's the matter?" Torme asked.

The chap smirked and replied that he had never seen such an ego trip for billing a show and performer.

Mel, not sure just what his friend was talking about, pressed his friend further.

"Quite carried away, aren't we?" the friend continued to jibe.

The matter was not clarified until the friend had been introduced to Rich Little. The friend had taken the marquee literally.

RICH LITTLE MEL TORME

★ ★ ★

Stunning film star Carole Lombard was flat-chested. Before any "take," she could be heard singing out to her wardrobe mistress:

"Okay! Bring me my breasts."

MAKE UP AND ACCESSORIES

★ ★ ★

The beautiful and fabulous Norma Talmadge, after starring in sixty movies and having garnered millions of fans, retired from the screen.

Some years later, when she came out of a Beverly Hills restaurant, a flock of movie buffs and fans were milling about. They spotted her and rushed toward her, but she escaped into her car. As she rolled up the window, she managed to shout a few words to the crowd. "Go away," she said. "I don't need you anymore!"

★ ★ ★

Before the advent of television, Paramount Studios installed a radio in the portrait gallery so that the star subjects being lighted and photographed could listen to background music. Mood music.

One day Mae West was the star being immortalized by the portrait photographer. Mae was tightly bound to properly show the wasp waist, large bosom above, and widely curved hips below.

This day was uncomfortably warm. Dear Mae was more so. At the time, there was no radio station that played only music; programs included comedy skits, talk sessions, and gag routines.

Mae was feeling playful, and she said to photographer Whitey Schafer, "You have retouchers, don't you?"

After the photographer acknowledged that he did, Mae reached into her dress and lifted out her right breast, then her left breast. "Who can take care of this?"

At that precise moment, the radio announcer came on loud and clear: "And now, introducing Mike and Ike."

Mae laughed loudest of all! Her gorgeous mammaries were thus christened.

★ ★ ★

★ ★ ★

One story about Marlene Dietrich has been told in several different versions, and has long been considered apochryphal. But it did happen, and it involved still photographer George Hurrell, not a motion picture cameraman as the story is most often told.

Early in Dietrich's career, Hurrell had taken some beautiful portrait shots of the star. Fifteen years later, at the peak of her international fame, she returned to Hurrell for more photographs.

After viewing the proofs, Marlene asked George, "Why is it that you don't seem to photograph me as well as you did fifteen years ago?"

Hurrell — ever the soul of discretion — replied, "I guess it's because I'm fifteen years older than I was then."

★ ★ ★

One anecdote concerning Marilyn Monroe has never been printed before. She may have been calling herself Norma Jean then, it's that far back. The time was just after World War II. Marilyn's close friend Robert Slatzer lived in a small house in the Hollywood Hills above Vine Street.

Down in Hollywood, Marilyn had a small apartment. The kitchen was larger than the bedroom. Alongside Marilyn's apartment was a driveway leading to a garage in the rear. In those days, something Bob and Marilyn shared was poverty; he was behind in his car payments, and she was four months behind in her rent.

The apartment manager had threatened to lock Marilyn out, holding her belongings until she paid the back rent. She called Bob Slatzer for aid and comfort, explaining her plight. As a good friend will do, he went immediatly to her apartment. It was raining, and he parked the car right outside her kitchen window.

Working quickly, Marilyn passed her belongings out the window, and Bob stowed them in the car. When they had finished, Bob crawled into the kitchen, and Marilyn poured them each a glass of scotch to toast her exit of a sticky situation.

Suddenly they heard a noise in the driveway, and Bob moved to the kitchen window to look out. His car was being backed down the drive into the street! Stolen! Along with all of Marilyn's worldly possessions. The two young folks climbed out the window and slipped away, walking three blocks to a pay phone to call the police station and report the theft.

The police informed them they would have to appear personally at the station to fill out forms.

They took a streetcar to the corner of Hollywood Boulevard and Vine Street. From there they hoofed it to the police station, filled out the forms, then walked back uphill to Bob's small house.

About two days later, Bob received a notice from the finance company that his car had been impounded, informing him that it would be released to him when the payments were made. The notice itemized a list of the items contained in the car.

Somehow, between Bob's and Marilyn's financial manipulations, and with small loans from several friends, Bob made the car payments, and it was returned to him.

"Hell," he commented, "They even had a tail on me in the middle of the rain!"

★ ★ ★

Actors Bill "Kit Carson" Williams and Richard "Captain Midnight" Webb, following a personal appearance in Hollywood, returned to Bill's home in the San Fernando Valley. There Bill's wife, Barbara Hale (of the *Perry Mason* television series), served them coffee and sandwiches.

About 2:00 A.M. Webb decided it was time to go home, but he couldn't get his car started. Williams offered his new MG. He tried to explain the gear shifts to Webb who vaguely understood. In a few minutes, about six blocks from Williams' house, the gears locked right in the middle of an intersection. A cruising police car stopped, and one of the officers walked to the stalled Webb — who was still in his Captain Midnight uniform and vainly attempting to operate the gears of the MG.

Webb: "Hi."

Officer: "Hi. (pause) This your car?"

Webb: "Nope."

Officer: "Whose is it?"

Webb: "Kit Carson's."

Pause.

Officer: "Who are you?"

Webb: "Captain Midnight."

Pause. The officer stepped closer to the car, flashed his light on Webb's face and on the uniform.

Officer: "By God! You are Captain Midnight!"

The police officers got Webb's autograph for their children, and showed him how to operate the gears.

★ ★ ★

When delightful June Allyson was married to Dick Powell, Metro-Goldwyn-Mayer cast her in a picture with Fred Astaire. Any actress would be delighted to work with Hollywood's all-time favorite dancer, but June was ecstatic. Fred had been her idol for years, and in this picture she would get to dance with him. That fact made her as nervous as she was happy.

When the day of the first dance rehearsals arrived, June felt butterflies in her stomach. By the time they had finished the first dance sequence on the set, this had grown to outright nausea, and June had to rush to her dressing room to throw up.

June tried everything she could think of to calm herself, but nothing worked. Every rehearsal was the same. After dancing with Fred Astaire, she would have to go to her dressing room to throw up. Finally a friend suggested that June should see a doctor to get a prescription for her queasy stomach.

Although Fred had been very patient and understanding with her, June was terribly embarrassed about the situation, so she decided to take her friend's advice. She told her sympathetic co-star about her plan.

After examining her, the doctor told June that nervousness was not the problem. She was pregnant, and she should not be performing the strenuous dance numbers, because it might endanger the baby. June was delighted with the news that she would be having a child, but she was upset that she would have to withdraw from the picture with Astaire.

As soon as she arrived home, June called Louis B. Mayer to tell him the problem. He was understanding and agreed to recast her part. Before hanging up, June asked if she could call Fred personally to explain and to apologize for the trouble. Mayer agreed. Of course June was nervous about doing this, but she felt it was the proper and respectful thing to do.

Quickly she dialed Fred's number. When he answered, she was so upset she didn't think to identify herself, but blurted out, "Mr. Astaire, I have something to tell you."

"Yes, what is it?" Fred asked.

"I'm pregnant!

There was a long pause at the other end of the line. Then Fred asked cautiously, "Who is this?"

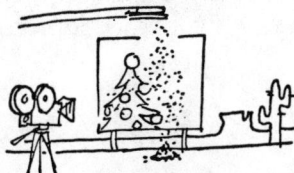

All stars are not vain about their appearance. In some cases, it is the studio heads who make rules about altering eyebrows, noses, mouths, or even ears.

When it was left up to him, Bing Crosby preferred to be himself, just a nice guy with a balding head and prominent ears. He didn't like wearing his toupee, and he didn't like having his ears pinned back by the makeup department. (The reason many old photos show him wearing a hat is that he preferred it to his toupee.) Because Bing frequently played romantic leads, the studio insisted on having a say regarding his appearance.

Wally Westmore was Bing's favorite makeup man. Wally knew just what had to be done for Bing before appearing on a set. The toupee was attached properly, and he applied the thin piece of elastic used to "pin back" the ears. This elastic was glued into place and hair was combed over it to hide it. It was a time-consuming procedure.

Wally did this work on Bing every day for one particular picture, and then was assigned to another film immediately after shooting was finished.

Then it was decided the film needed some more shots — about twenty of them, all close-ups of Bing, which were to be interspersed with other scenes throughout the picture. Bing was called back, but Wally could not do the makeup, so another artist was assigned to prepare the star. Naturally, Bing didn't mention the ears.

The scenes were shot and edited into place.

When the picture was released, audiences responded with much laughter at the unintended special effects. Throughout the film, Bing's ears appeared to be flapping, as if they were wings of a bird preparing to take flight.

★ ★ ★

★ ★ ★

An older film star — whose name we will graciously omit — was making a film after many years absence from the screen. She was still a great actress, but after such a long period of inactivity she was having difficulty remembering her lines. To help her out, director and crew devised a way of feeding the dialogue to her. They rigged up a small radio receiver in her ear, hiding it from the view of the camera.

This worked fine until one day when a police traffic helicopter flew over the studio broadcasting on the same frequency being used by the director.

In the middle of her dialogue the actress announced, "There's a traffic pile-up at the intersection of Highland and Santa Monica."

★ ★ ★

When the studio system was in its decline in Hollywood, Ricardo Montalban was one of the last of the term contract players to be released from MGM. He had been accustomed to a comfortable weekly income, with a lovely home in the Santa Monica mountains and his children in private schools. No longer under contract, he sat by the phone waiting for offers for film roles, but none were forthcoming.

Finally his agent called to report on an offer to make a costume epic, *The Death of Bathsheba*, in Italy. Knowing the reputation of the Italian epics of the period, Ricardo turned it down.

Another month or two passed, and there were still no other offers. *The Death of Bathsheba* began to look more attractive, so the actor called his agent to ask if the role was still open. It was. If the terms were good, he told his agent, he would accept the work.

The experience wasn't as bad as Ricardo had expected, and it was good to be able to continue working. He finished the picture and came home. Again months went by and there were no offers for films in the United States, so the actor called his agent to ask if there might be another role for him in Italy. His agent checked and called back a few days later to convey a new offer for a picture being made in Rome.

While making the film in Rome, Ricardo was having lunch one day with a friend at an outdoor cafe. Suddenly the actor noticed an ostentatiously effeminate man staring at him. The man was dressed flamboyantly in wild colors, and he had flaming red hair. Ricardo was used to being recognized and approached by fans, so he was not particularly disturbed as the stranger swept toward him.

Approaching the table, however, the man gushed loudly: "Ohhh, Mr. Monntallbaaan, it's reeeelly you! I've always thought you were just wonnnderfull! I just haave to indroduce myself, because I was the one who dubbed your voice in *The Death of Bathsheeeba!*"

★ ★ ★

Mae West was doing a Paramount picture, and she approached director Raoul Walsh one day to ask a favor. "I've got this friend, Kid Moreno, a prize fighter," she told him. "He's down on his luck and can use a job. I'd like you to give him a scene with a line of dialogue."

Walsh granted the favor, and Moreno was given a scene in which he was to come to Mae's room to say, "There's a boatload of guns down in the harbor."

Mae was to reply, "Bring 'em ashore. We'll open a sporting store, and you can run it."

Then Moreno was to exit. It was a simple scene, but the prize fighter was anxious about doing a good job. During lunchtime, comedian Walter Catlett helped him to rehearse.

When it came time to shoot the scene, Kid Moreno had his line down perfectly. However, he was still nervous. While the cameras were running, he came into Mae's room and announced, "There's a boatload of cunts down in the harbor."

Ever the quick-witted professional, Mae replied immediately, "Bring 'em ashore. We'll open a sportin' house, and you can play the piano."

★ ★ ★

W.C. Fields was not noted for his modesty. When he was shooting on the back lot of Paramount, he saw no need to walk the one and a half blocks to the men's room. His favorite spot to relieve himself was a pleasant green area, backed by nicely kept shrubs. When he was so moved, he would walk over to this area, turn to face the company (who were in full view), drop his trousers, and squat down.

This was not only an embarrassment for the cast and crew, who had to pretend they didn't see, but it was also an annoyance for the "Green Man," who had the responsibility for keeping the studio grounds clean and attractive. It seemed never to occur to Fields that someone would have to clean up after him.

Of course the Green Man could not protest to the great star, but he decided to do something in his own quiet way to resolve the problem.

One morning as Fields squatted and the cast tried not to notice, the Green Man hid in the bushes behind the comedian. At the appropriate moment, a long-handled shovel was extended quietly from the bushes and held strategically suspended until Fields had finished. Then it was just as quietly pulled back to be disposed of.

After he had pulled up his trousers, buttoned his fly, and arranged his clothes, Fields turned to check the deposit he had made before returning to the set.

There was nothing there. He started to walk away, then turned and came back to the site, with a baffled expression on his face. Then a look of horror came over him, and he reached his hand back to feel the seat of his pants. He was clearly relieved to feel nothing amiss.

He walked back to the set muttering and shaking his head in astonishment. Throughout the morning, when he was between scenes, he would return to the spot, scouring the area, talking to himself and shaking his head in disbelief.

No one ever told him what had happened.

★ ★ ★

One apocryphal story made the rounds of the studios for many years. It concerned a Jewish character actor in his eighties, who was on his deathbed. He was tended constantly by his daughter.

"Would you do me a favor?" he asked weakly, knowing his hours were numbered.

"Yes, Papa," his daughter replied. "What is it?"

"I can tell by the smell that your mother is making strudel," he said. "Please, I want one little piece."

His daughter went out and returned a moment later to tell him apologetically, "Mama says no."

"But why?" he asked. "It can't do me any harm now. I'm dying."

His daughter explained, "Mama says it's for after the funeral."

★ ★ ★

John Barrymore once made a film in which there appeared a delightfully talented chimpanzee named George. During the filming, Barrymore became very fond of George. The actor and the chimp became so attached they were virtually inseparable.

As the filming was drawing to a close, Barrymore

realized that he was going to miss George terribly, so he approached the chimp's owner/trainer and explained, "I really love George, and I'd like to buy him."

The owner smiled and asked, "How much money do you make?"

"Three thousand dollars a week," Barrymore replied, not sure why the man was asking.

Still smiling, George's owner told him, "George loves you, too. He makes five thousand a week and would like to buy you."

★ ★ ★

John and Ethel Barrymore were doing a play together on Broadway. Opening night was a great success, and the press flocked backstage to interview the two members of the great American theatrical family. Because brother and sister were working together, naturally the reporters asked questions related to family.

John and Ethel had dressing rooms next to each other, but divided by a partition. While Ethel changed, John received the press, allowing them to ask questions as he removed his makeup.

One reporter turned the interview to the subject of the Barrymores' uncle, John Drew, who had recently died. "What was the last play Mr. Drew starred in?" the reporter asked.

John couldn't recall, so he shouted over the partition to Ethel, "Dear, what was the last thing Uncle John was in?"

Immediately Ethel shouted back, "I think it was that little redheaded ingenue named Georgia!"

★ ★ ★

★ ★ ★

The competition between Bob Hope and Bing Crosby was a running gag for many years. The two men were very close friends, but there was a slight degree of truth to their banter. Although he did not wish to admit it openly, Bob did not like to be topped or bested by Bing, who always got first billing when they worked together.

At the height of their popularity as a comedy team, *The Saturday Evening Post* did a six-installment series about the life of Crosby, as told to Pete Martin, who was their star reporter. The articles proved to be very successful.

About a year later, the *Post* wanted to do the same with Bob Hope, again using Pete Martin and again printing in six installments.

Aware that this might require some delicate negotiations, Martin called Teet Carle to make the request. When Carle passed along the offer to Hope, the comedian agreed, with one stipulation — the series would have to run in seven installments.

★ ★ ★

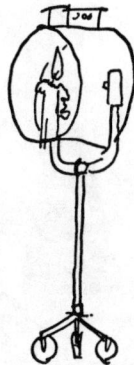

Jeff Corey, a most excellent actor, is a good mimic. Early in his career, he was hired for a demanding role in *True Grit*. In one scene the director's idea for playing out the scene was quite different from the concept Jeff had in mind. The director "walked" the scene, Jeff observing closely. The director showed Jeff exactly how he wanted the movement played, how he wanted the facial expressions done, and what sort of nuances of action and reaction he sought.

Then he called for the take. Jeff did everything just as the director had laid it out for him.

"Cut," the director ordered! "No, no. That's not the way to do it!" he commanded.

"I did it just like you did, sir," Jeff explained. He was on the spot, in front of cast and crew, and he felt he had to extricate himself from the director's disfavor.

"Hell," the director snorted. "I'm not an actor."

★ ★ ★

From the great W. C. Fields on the subject of you-know-what: "There may be things better than sex, there may be things worse than sex, but there's nothing *exactly* like it."

★ ★ ★

Joan Crawford came to Hollywood in the late 1920s, a well-trained, experienced dancer from New York. She knew she had to find a showplace for fast recognition and learned that, on Friday evenings, the Cocoanut Grove at the Ambassador Hotel held "college nights."

Every Friday night Joan appeared with a boy friend whose first attribute was being a good dancer. Every week she won the silver cup for performing the dance crazes of the day: the Black Bottom and the Charleston and several twists and turns of her own invention.

However, the real college crowd finally rose up in indignation and protest. She was no co-ed! She was a professional, and they wanted something done about her! Give the college girls, the real ones, a chance.

The crowds of on-lookers loved Joan, but the hotel wanted to hold onto the college trade. The management decided to keep everyone happy by each week awarding three cups. Always one of them went to Joan Crawford.

★ ★ ★

Laura Hope Crews, for decades a celebrated stage and screen star, and still to be seen on television as Aunt Pittypat in *Gone With The Wind* (among other films) was also famous for helping many eager young thespians in their careers. Alfred Lunt is one she assisted. Fredric March another.

Once, many summers ago, a young girl desiring to be an actress had to resort to selling tickets for the plays at the Cape Playhouse in Dennis, Massachusetts. Laura Hope Crews was directing as well as starring in the play, *Mr. Pim Passes By*. However, no member of the stock company of actors quite fitted Miss Crews' idea of the daughter's role.

She had met the girl who sold the tickets in the box

office, and she persuaded her to read for the ingenue role. The young girl was cast in the part and did very well during the run of the play. Perhaps as well as in subsequent roles and in a few memorable Hollywood films. She did many roles in radio dramas, and when television came along she did a role or four or six or ten, continuing to act in theater and films, lend her support as well to many charities and professional functions.

Who was Miss Crews' discovery?

Miss Bette Davis.

★ ★ ★

Tallulah Bankhead's first Hollywood film was *The Devil And The Deep* at Paramount. One evening, out on the town, she startled and pleased a crowd at a sleazy night-spot by performing the Dance of the Seven Veils; all very much private fun and not something to read about the next morning.

However, the next day a reporter from the *Los Angeles Examiner* showed up at the studio asking to see Miss Tallulah. The publicists tried to steer him away, but the star said, "Hell, I'll handle it. Bring him on!"

Miss Bankhead greeted the reporter. "I'm glad that your paper checks false stories like this," she said. "Why a false story would cause me to have to sue for libel, as I've had to do three times against the careless press in London. I suppose you saw that I recently won six thousand pounds from one paper in England. I had to prove I don't like untrue stories about myself, dahling!

"Now, about this story you have heard. . . . "

The story never got in print.

★ ★ ★

★ ★ ★

The cello voice of the impeccable Ethel Barymore dominated any conversation. She was the grand expert at turning the caustic remark — or turning any remark caustic, as the case may be.

Lady Ethel was informed that a certain female entertainer, noted for a mouth that would not stop at any obscenities, had been booked into a cavernous theater where chances were she'd never be heard by much of the audience.

"Good," Miss Barrymore replied with a smile. "At last she can be obscene but not heard!"

★ ★ ★

V
WRITERS
&
AUTHORS

"'The question is,' said Alice,
'whether you can make words
mean so many things.'"

Over objections of executives of Columbia Studios' sales department, who reported that fantasy pictures were box-office poison, Harry Cohn permitted the making of *Here Comes Mr. Jordan*. The project was the story of a man (played by Robert Montgomery) who returns to earth after his death.

When the film was released, it was a huge success. It won Academy Awards for writing for George Axelrod, and gathered several Academy nominations, including best picture, best direction, and best cinematography.

Later, when George Axelrod met with Harry Cohn and tried to sell Columbia a fantasy script he had written, the mogul said to Axelrod, "No Way! Fantasy always flops."

Axelrod cited the great success of *Mr. Jordan*.

"True," Cohn retorted. "But just imagine how much more it might have made if it hadn't been a fantasy."

★ ★ ★

Bennett Cerf, recording in his *Saturday Review* column, wrote of a writer with an outstanding reputation for Broadway successes. The writer was given a contract by a top Hollywood producer. When he turned in his first scenario, the head of the studio called the writer's agent. "We're not taking up his option," the agent was informed. "You'd better get rid of him, too. He's such a highbrow."

The agent was surprised. He inquired further.

"I'll bet he writes failures on purpose," the mogul said.

★ ★ ★

Before his years of success as a producer, Norman Krasna was a young writer and well known for bright quips and retorts. In a screening room at Warner Brothers one day someone remarked at the conclusion of viewing a new film soon to be released: "Well, it needs a little cutting."

"Sure," Krasna added, "Right down the middle and be sure to throw both halves away."

★ ★ ★

Dashiell Hammett and Ben Hecht, both popular writers of best-selling novels, made it to Hollywood, anticipating becoming rich, if not eminent, screen writers. Hammett liked to tell about the time before he began writing his novels, when he had a real detective agency (*a la* Sam Spade of *The Maltese Falcon*). And young Hecht, a newspaperman with writing ambitions, sought a job as a prime sleuth, to gain experience.

"You couldn't survive," Hammett challenged Hecht. "Suppose you were in your car and another car, full of hoods, suddenly came charging at your car at seventy miles an hour. What would you do?"

"Eighty!" Hecht replied.

★ ★ ★

★ ★ ★

Many years ago, the head of a major Hollywood studio employed an efficiency expert, instructing that all working situations on the lot be investigated, and that any necessary corrections be made. During the second week of the investigations, the efficiency expert stormed into the mogul's office, red-faced, and with a ghastly report. "I was attracted by paper clips falling from a third story window of the Writer's Building. I investigated and found a man who said he was a writer. But he was not writing! He said he was thinking while he flipped paper clips toward the window.

"So I told him he must stop this game instantly. I told him to get to work on his typewriter. He told me to go screw a duck! Well, I was furious. So I told him I was coming directly over to you to report his behavior, and do you know what he said? He said I should tell you for him that you could crap in your hat!"

The studio chief was livid. "Who is this man?" he shouted. Mr. Expert named the writer, and Mr. Mogul sat back down on his chair with a thud.

"Well, what are we going to do about this?" the efficiency expert demanded.

"That man happens to have written nothing but box-office smash hits for us during the past three years," the mogul said. "He's never failed." He sighed deeply, resigning himself to his fate. "Well, I've got the hat," the mogul said. "I suggest you go look for a duck!"

★ ★ ★

There was another movie mogul who paid a bundle for the screen rights to a smash hit play. The chore of transposing the stage work into a viable, moving screenplay was assigned to a very successful scenarist, who was also paid a bundle.

When the scenario for the film was turned in, the producer bellowed loud and clear, "What a gyp! My God, the plot of the screenplay is exactly like the stage play."

★ ★ ★

The author and newspaperman, Leo Guild, recalled the day a screenwriter (whose filmscript had been in production about a week at Warner Brothers) was seated in a studio projection room with Jack Warner. There were present a few friends watching the scenes of the film that had been shot. They were awful, woefully so.

When the projections were completed, the lights went up, and Jack Warner stood. "I want to see you in my office in ten minutes," he told the screenwriter.

Quite soon thereafter, as the writer and friends made their way through the hallways toward the Warner office, they were acutely aware of a heavy rainstorm outside, with a good deal of wind and lightning. Suddenly, all the lights in the building dimmed and fluttered.

"What's that?" asked a friend.

"It must be Mr. Warner testing the chair," the writer said sullenly.

★ ★ ★

★ ★ ★

The actor and writer Irvin S. Cobb has related a story of the studio head whose opinion of a particular story line was in sharp disagreement with one of his eager young staff members. "From now on," the mogul shouted to his underling, "whenever you talk to me you keep your mouth shut!"

★ ★ ★

Having mentioned seats and seatings, we should give equal time to Herman J. Mankiewicz's caustic brand of personalized humor, which could humble the most haughty of bosses, somehow eliciting smiles, even when barbs were thrown right into their laps.

One who did not appreciate being the butt of the writer's repartee was Columbia's Harry Cohn. Mankiewicz received a screenwriting assignment at Columbia, and the producer of the film asked Herman not to risk angering Cohn by eating in the studio cafe where Cohn always swapped words with high-ranking studio personnel.

Mankiewicz was unable to resist the no-no, and he showed up at the executive table one noon. He really did not want to upset Cohn, but fate played another, heavy hand. Herman listened incredulously as King Harry explained how it was not necessary for him to see a movie in a theater with a live audience. "I sit in my projection room, and my fanny tells me what's good, what's bad. If my fanny muscles get taut and I have to squirm about the seat, I know the film is lousy. If I can sit and my fanny behaves, I know I'm viewing a winner."

Silence ensued until Mankiewicz's voice spilled over the table and surrounded all of those present. "My God, how sad. Our whole world is wired to Harry Cohn's ass."

—124—

★ ★ ★

Sidney Buchman was a fair-haired boy with Harry Cohn because he wrote scripts for a number of Columbia Picture's biggest hits. Cohn even granted Buchman singlecard credit on the main titles. However, King Cohn constantly berated the writer for not obeying his demands that all employees, including writers, keep regular 9:00 A.M. to 6:00 P.M. office hours.

Buchman's argument was that writers were not machines, and talent could not be regulated within just that time frame. He told Cohn he should stop having in-and-out checklists made on his creative employees. But then, Cohn insisted if he let his pal Buchman get by with irregular hours, it would be a bad example for all the other employees on the lot.

For a few days Buchman managed the 9-to-6 route, working on a script assignment and reporting directly to Cohn. But after a few more days of those routine hours, Cohn complained that Buchman was not having success solving a sticky story point.

Buchman's reply was to say that he had come up with a perfect solution to the story problem, but unfortunately he could not use it in this script he was writing. "It came to me just last night," Buchman told Cohn. "While I was taking a shower — on my own time, not on the 9-to-6 time span you pay me for. Now if you paid me for my creative thoughts for a film project, no matter when my ideas came, instead of only what popped into my mind while in my office on the lot. . . ."

Sidney Buchman kept his own hours from then on!

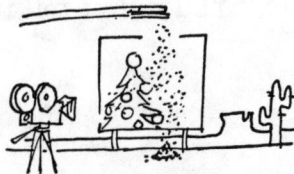

★ ★ ★

The screenwriters under contract at Paramount in the 1950s had a special table at the studio commissary where they gathered for lunch. Telling jokes and funny stories became a regular part of their mealtime routine. Since they saw each other every day, the jokes were often repeated, but favorites always prompted laughter time after time. Eventually the writers knew all the stories so well that one of their group suggested they ought to assign numbers to them so they wouldn't have to go to the trouble of retelling them. All they would have to do was announce a number, and everyone would laugh.

One day a new writer joined the studio in a junior position, and he was invited to join their lunch-table. He was bewildered by what took place. One of the old-hands would say gleefully, "Eight," and everybody would laugh. Then another would break in with "Twenty-two," and there would be more delighted guffaws. He felt very much an outsider, but he did not want to ask what was going on, because that would be a public admission that he was a novice.

After several days of the same routine, the new writer asked a trusted associate to explain. Wanting to feel a part of the in-group, the young man decided to join in the joke-telling at lunch that day. At an appropriate pause in the laughter, he mustered his courage and announced, "Fifteen!"

There was no laughter. Everybody stared at him somberly.

After lunch, as the group walked back to the writer's building, the novice asked his trusted associate why no one had laughed at his joke.

He was informed, "You didn't tell it right."

★ ★ ★

★ ★ ★

One of the most colorful of the early Hollywood writers was a man named Grover Jones. He had little formal education, but he had a long career that began in the silent era and lasted well into the period of talkies. His first job, however, was as a sign-painter on the back lot of the old Universal Studios.

Painting signs was not a particularly challenging or creative job for a man of Grover's talents, but he turned it into one. Assigned to paint all the signs and display windows of the storefronts of the Western street, he turned a tedious task into fun. As a way of saying hello to all the folks back in his small mid-western hometown, he decided to use their names on the establishments of the Western set.

When one of the Westerns filmed on the set reached his hometown, all hell broke loose. The citizens of the town — the Mayor, the Police Chief, the ministers, the schoolteachers — did not appreciate having their names on undertaking parlors, saloons, corset shops, and fertilizer supply stores.

To cap it all off, one obvious bordello bore the name of a prominent local belle.

★ ★ ★

★ ★ ★

When the celebrated Dorothy Parker signed a writing contract with MGM, her reputation as one of the great literary figures of New York preceded her. The studio assigned her a private office with a door, and the other writers kept a respectful distance from the woman who was known for her biting wit.

Dorothy's rebellious spirit refused to accept this solitary confinement. She had not been at MGM very long before she devised a plan. When no one was about, she went down the hall and removed the sign from the men's room door and placed it on the door of her office.

She quickly made many friends.

★ ★ ★

Whether they admit it publicly or not, authors of books aspire to great revenues from the sale of their works to motion pictures. Although many of Hollywood's greatest films could not have been made without the books, the authors don't always do as well as they expect. Sometimes the film sale works out to the detriment of the writer.

Take the example of H. Allen Smith, who wrote the novel *Rhubarb*, from which the picture of the same name was made.

He sold the rights to his book to a minor producer for $20,000, with the provision that he would get half the amount over that if the producer resold it. That is, he was to get half, after any expenses were deducted.

The producer sold the rights to Paramount for $45,000. Smith expected to receive $12,500, perhaps minus a few thousand. Not so. The producer drew up a list of expenses that totalled $27,500 (which included $5,000 for legal fees and another $5,000 for a script). He claimed to be losing $2,500 on the deal, and Smith had to accept it.

The clincher Smith put into a letter to his friend Rufus Blair, of Paramount's publicity department. A number of his friends had not bought copies of the book *Rhubarb*, all with the same excuse — "I don't want to read the book because it might spoil the movie for me."

★ ★ ★

H. Allen Smith was also a gentleman. He believed in treating all people with respect, regardless of race, creed, color, or station in life. Sometimes that could be difficult, as he reported in another letter to publicity man Rufus Blair.

"The Pullman porter came in," he wrote from the train, "and I asked him what his name was because I have a terrible complex about calling all porters George, as folks do. And he says, 'George.' I said Jesus Christ Amiday. 'You mean to say your name is really George?' and he says it is. So I say I refuse to call no porter George so you'd better tell me your last name so I can call you by that. He says, 'My name in full, is George Smith.' I give up."

★ ★ ★

By now everyone knows about the close relationship between mystery writer Dashiell Hammett and playwright Lillian Hellman. The two of them spent some time — separately and simultaneously — working on scripts for Hollywood movies, even though their greatest successes were not in tinseltown.

Hellman has given Hammett much credit for guiding her in her writing. One story she often related was about the writing of her play, *The Autumn Garden*. After reading the first draft of this effort, Hammett criticized it so strongly that Hellman destroyed it and started over.

After finishing the second draft, Hellman again gave it

to Hammett to read. This time the mystery writer approved of it — everything except a speech in the last act. The playwright refused to do any more work.

The play was set for production, with Harold Clurman directing. During rehearsals, Clurman asked for the speech to be rewritten. Lillian Hellman gave it another try. The result still was not satisfactory. Throughout the rehearsal period she rewrote the speech several times, but the director was never satisfied. Finally, just before the opening, Clurman was pleased with a last-ditch effort. To the playwright, he praised it highly, telling her it was very good.

Hellman nodded. "It should be," she said. "Dashiell Hammett wrote it."

During the dark days of the McCarthy Era, a great many writers were blacklisted in Hollywood, along with quite a few actors and actresses, because of suspected communist leanings. Because the writers were relatively powerless, fear ran through the writing departments of most studios.

No doubt Jack Warner was attempting to resolve this fear when he announced to his writing department, "They'll never find a blacklist at Warner Brothers. Here, everything is done on the phone."

★ ★ ★

★ ★ ★

In recent years, the art of writing has undergone a great many changes. Rules and tools have been dropped in a process of simplification. Whether this is from choice or lack of education we will leave to others to determine. One of the tools that has fallen by the wayside is the simile, to the regret of many who delight in the more playful aspects of language.

At one time similes were the stock in trade of publicists, columnists, and screenwriters, who enjoyed quoting not only their own best efforts but also those of their peers. Frank J. Wilstach went so far as to collect the best and most amusing of similes from the 1920s and 1930s, publishing them in his *Dictionary of Similes*, which became a reference for writers and publicists in Hollywood.

A sampling from Wilstach's collection follows:

"The rain came down with swift, slanting strokes, like the penmanship of an old schoolteacher."
> — Gene Fowler

"Difficult to detect as perspiration on a fish."
> — Merville Hammet

"Crooked as a man who double-crosses his Ts."
> — Joseph Hill

"Fleeting as the fame of an English Channel swimmer."
> — Barrett Kiesling

"Hampered, like a man trying to whistle while holding his breath."
> — Westbrook Pegler

"He had as many aliases as a hotel register."
> — John P. Stack

"She looked as new as a peeled egg."
                    — Dorothy Parker

"Arguing with the wife is like lathering a mirror and shaving your reflection."
                    — Arthur "Bugs" Baer

"She kissed him with the warmth of one sticking a stamp on a letter."
                    — Dorothy Black

"Busy as a female centipede crossing her legs."
                    — Ide Gruber

"Difficult as it is for a one-legged man to put his best foot forward."
                    — Arthur James

"She was as thin as a rolled umbrella."
                    — Clifford Orr

"Reluctant as a newspaper retraction."
                    — Carlton Andrews

"She was so thin her gown looked as though it hung from a nail."
                    — Anonymous

"Contented as a movie actor in a Hall of Mirrors."
                    — Anonymous

"As uncomfortable as a sword swallower with the hiccoughs."
                    — Anonymous

★ ★ ★

VI
PROMOTERS
&
PUBLICISTS

"All a publicist can do is get
the picture an opening. After
that, the film's gotta have legs
for a long run."

★ ★ ★

Hollywood Publicists have been termed "colorful" and "inventive." Sometimes, they are discoverers of talent, but always they reflect what is good or bad in their clients — the producers, directors, stars, and such, for whom they must labor. Their main task is to be sure their clients' names are constantly before the public in newspaper stories and in the columns that tell all there is to tell about the famous and the infamous. If a vote had been taken a few years ago among newspaper editors around the country, the winner of the Publicists' Prize would probably have been an estimable chap named Rufus Blair.

Rufus worked principally for Paramount Studios. His real name was Marvin, but in his early twenties, in San Francisco, his flaming red hair gave him the nickname of "Rufus," and he adopted it. Although lured to Hollywood, Rufus had a lifelong love affair with the Bay City. During the major part of his career as a publicity expert, he had direct contact with every movie journalist in the United States. The press knew and adored the man. He helped many of them to come to Hollywood to do their articles on movieland and moviepeople for their hometown papers.

Typical of a San Franciscan, Rufus Blair had little love for Los Angeles. Hollywood was okay with him, but Los Angeles was a dirty name. He capitalized on this attitude. Each week, Rufus sent an "exclusive" story (with photos) to newspapers in the country's key cities.

A mimeographed letter accompanied each publicity release. Sensing that midwestern and eastern newsmen who sniffled and coughed their way through hard winters were angered by the sunshine-and-paradise attitude coming from the other publicists in Los Angeles, Rufus began early to write disparaging things about L. A. Always, of course, the publicity release accompanying the form letter contained a plug of one kind or another for the film he was pushing, or for its actors and actresses. All over the nation the editors who received his epistles chose to print them in toto. Their readers — who also resented the smugness of Tinseltown, America — loved them. It has taken many years for the Los Angeles Chamber of Commerce and the office of tourism to overcome the attitudes his releases encouraged.

Rufus began his letters by alluding to digging his way out of the debris of flash floods, canyon fires, and earthquake rubble. When smog filled L. A. air, Rufus had an everlasting peg. He had been date-lining his letter from "Double-Dubuque." Now he had them emanate from Smogsville, or Vista Del Smog. He christened the Dodger baseball team the *Smodgers*.

Some of Rufus Blair's humor was hilarious, but sometimes hilarious things happened to Rufus. For instance, on one of his trips around the country, he landed in Louisville, Kentucky, only to find there was no room to be had. It was Derby time. (He could not believe anyone would travel from faraway places just to see horses run around a track.) He taxied across the river to Cincinnati, Ohio. That city was full up, too! He would not be denied a night's sleep, so he demanded the cabbie drop him in front of the biggest hospital in town.

There, he signed in as a patient, informing them that a Doctor Holmes would be doing some tests the following day. Came the dawn, and he was awakened for a sponge bath. At this point, he confessed all, paid his bill (hospital rooms were cheap in those days), and left a staff of nurses and clerks wagging their astonished heads.

On another occasion, Rufus ended a week of plugging a picture in San Francisco. He enjoyed a wonderful prime rib dinner with newspaper pals, after which he wrapped the succulent bone in a large napkin. He would take it back home to Hollywood to his dog, Fagin. That night in his hotel room he stowed the wrapped bone in a bureau drawer.

The next morning he received a wire from the studio, telling him to stay on for six days more in order to do some work. He forgot the bone until the day came to leave. (By that time, a strange odor in the room assailed his nostrils.)

On the way out of the hotel on a brief errand he carried the napkin-wrapped bone with him, found a convenient broom closet, and stashed it there. That afternoon when he returned, the entire floor of the hotel was cordoned off, alive with lawmen. He was allowed to go to his room where he hastily fumigated it with a cologne spray. With his assignment completed, he prepared to check out of the hotel. While he was paying his bill, the hotel manager came up to him and asked, "Why did you do such a thing to us?"

Rufus tried to look innocently inquisitive. "Oh, we found the bone," the manager continued. "By smell, of course. The police and the FBI were called in to do lab work, to see if it was human — if murder had been committed. The maid reported that same smell in your room.

"We know you were the one to put the bone in the broom closet. From now on, Mr. Blair," the manager concluded, "take your business and your bones to some other hotel."

★ ★ ★

A true Hollywood story concerns the movie producing team of Bill Pine and Bill Thomas — and their bout with what has been called "The Incident of the Parrots." It happened when they ran the advertising-exploitation department at Paramount Studios in the early thirties.

Paramount produced a Mae West starrer entitled *It Ain't No Sin*. Fifty parrots were purchased by the two Bills, and every day the luckless birds were taken to the recording room at the studio and subjected for hours to a tape endlessly repeating, "It ain't no sin." In time the birds were saying "It ain't no sin" in their sleep!

The training went on for two weeks, but then the studio changed the film's title to *I'm No Angel*.

Immediately the publicity idea that was "great" had no use, and the result was fifty unemployed one-liner parrots. But publicists are ingenious. To get some additional track for the Mae West film, the department pens released a story that the fifty parrots had been flown to Central America and released in the jungle. There, in various sized choral groups, or single solo, they could continue to chant to the trees and animals: "It ain't no sin. It ain't no sin!" Until a new generation could begin language lessons.

★ ★ ★

Louella Parsons, the columnist whose words of Hollywood wisdom and happenings appeared in all the "right" newspapers, especially those owned by William Randolph Hearst, gave an account in one *Los Angeles Examiner* column of an all-night party that began with a Marion Davies world premiere.

"Lolly" wrote: "Marion never looked lovelier. As indeed she did at the lavish supper that followed, and at the Director's home where she danced until five; and then to her beach house where all of her hundred guests were invited for a champagne breakfast . . . and as the sun came up over the Pacific and the weary but heart-warmed friends were taking their leave, after a night they would never forget, there stood the fresh-eyed hostess in a charming little morning frock bidding each farewell. And Marion, dear Marion, never looked *slovener*." (Author italics)

The *Los Angeles Times* columnist, Hedda Hopper, caught the slip and watched her own star rise in the *west* as Louella's sun faded in the *east*.

★ ★ ★

Bernie Kamins, now a publicity consultant, began his career in 1940 as a junior publicist at Paramount Studios. Young Kamins' first assignment was as a unit publicist on the *Hopalong Cassidy* western series of films, being produced by Harry "Pop" Sherman and starring William Boyd. The films were made at the old California Studios in Hollywood, then owned by Paramount.

Bernie Kamins was fresh out of Harvard University and didn't know buttons from bows about a western film, the west itself, nor horses, their riders and history, nor how to write publicity about it all. Instead of taking a Sunday off, being eager to grasp his job, he would go to the publicity department of the studio and study all the materials written by others, particularly the stories and releases of his predecessor, Walter Bradfield. In one mimeographed release by Bradfield, Bernie came upon the word "cowpike." (On the typewriter keyboard the "o" and the "i" are next to each other, so Bernie's view was hindered by inexperience with typographical errors.)

Kamins knew that all of Bradfield's material was published throughout the country and so what he read must be right. In preparing his material for the *Hopalong Cassidy* horse operas Bernie called cowpokes, "cowpikes."

The department copy editor was not particularly fond of — nor charitable toward — college boys. Rather than correct Mr. Kamins' material he went to his superior, the director of publicity, George Brown. The editor complained specifically because young Kamins' stories had gone directly from California Studios to the press — Hopalong Cassidy was a "cowpike."

Not long after this, Jesse Spiro of the *Cleveland Plain Dealer*, a fine reporter with a fine paper, visited Hollywood. At Paramount he asked to see George Brown. He pulled a newspaper from his pocket and asked Brown, "What the hell is a cowpike?" Spiro, formerly an English teacher, told Brown he had been through every dictionary and synonym book and could not find the word.

Nonplussed, Brown asked an assistant for the definition, at the same time defending Kamins to Spiro. "Look, Jesse, the boy is a Harvard man. If he says it's cowpike, it's cowpike, goddamit!"

Within a few hours, a memorandum was tacked onto the bulletin board of the Paramount publicity department.

To: All publicity department personnel:
Please note:
    "Cowpike" — A Jewish cowboy.

★ ★ ★

Tallulah Bankhead was introduced to the unique methods Hollywood columnists employ when she told a visiting news-hen that she, Tallulah, had a personal chatter item about herself to give to the lady columnist.

Suprise! The lady refused to hear it; politely of course. "Sorry, but I never accept gossip items about important stars. I prefer to make up my own chatter for my column. So I know that what I write *is* exclusive!"

★ ★ ★

One publicist, Mike Kaplan, used every means possible to get mention in the columns for any film he was assigned to promote. He invented actors and actresses for odd roles in a picture he handled. He received space for 27 such "dreams," but then he was startled near the end of the film's production to receive a memorandum from the company's New York office: "We're preparing press kits and must include biographies of all the film's players. We have noted there are twenty-seven actors in the picture on whom you have done no biographies. We need them all within a week."

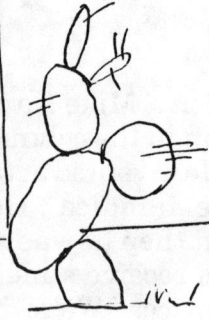

★ ★ ★

Teet Carle joins the continuing world interest in W. C. Fields. Why not? The great man gave Teet a hand-up in his budding career. It happened in September, 1927, when in his own words. . .

I had visited some newspaper friends, then publicity men at Paramount Studios, for lunch. I wondered why Harold Hurley, assistant publicity director, whom I had not met before, asked me so many questions about my job as sports publicity director at the University of Southern California.

The next day Hurley called and offered me a job. I would be on probation for two months, he said. If I clicked, I would become a junior publicist, with a $10 a week raise — or be out looking for another job.

The day I reported to Paramount I was handed a silent movie script of a picture called *Two Flaming Youths*. The picture starred W. C. Fields and Chester Conklin. I was assigned the task of obtaining a full biography of the star, W. C. Fields. The picture was already in production, shooting for a week. I was to be driven to the location of the production, a small village set at the old Paramount ranch in the San Fernando Valley, at Calabasas, California.

I arrived at the location just after lunch. Despite the fact that Fields had long worked on Broadway and in vaudeville, and had starred for Paramount at their Long Island studios in *Sally of The Sawdust, Poppy, So's Your Old Man, Running Wild*, and *The Old Army Game*, the studio had only a 600-word story of Field's career and life. To this day, I don't know how they had missed doing a biography.

When I arrived at the location, I checked in with the assistant director, told him I was to talk with Fields and gather as much information as I could to write a biography.

The young AD was more than friendly; he was enthusiastic. There had been a mix up in the shooting schedule and Fields would not appear before the camera until late in the day. The staff had been anticipating some thundering invectives from Fields because of the delay. The assistant pointed out a solitary figure in a rocking chair on a false front veranda set, fanning himself. It was Fields.

The day was blistering hot. He scowled ferociously as I approached. "Good afternoon, Mr. Fields," I said. "I'm Teet Carle, the publicity man."

He lit up like a Christmas tree. He beamed. "What did you say your name is?"

"It's Teet — a nickname. My real name is Cecil."

That did it. He instructed me to pull up another rocker and we went on talking. "I hated my name," he said. "William Claude Dukenfeld. For myself, my nickname is 'Whitey'."

He opened up quickly, telling me incredible stories about his "growing up" and his long career. In the conversation, he got around to his interest in names and naming. He delighted in the names he had come upon in southern California, like Agoura, Malibu, and the coastal Point Magu and Hueneme. He savored the sounds that fell through the teeth and past the lips, and he relaxed.

I told of working on a newspaper in Pomona; I had been in Azusa and Cucamonga. He asked me if that's where kumquats grew. We tossed around such places as Simi, Pacoima, Reseda, Encino, Tarzana, Tujunga, Winnetka, Sylmar, and Canoga. (In 1927 all of these locations and names seemed very remote and small and unimportant except, perhaps for the sounds pouring out of the mouth of W. C. Fields.)

I endeared myself to him when I said I'd been born in a town called Emporia, in a state that had places like Olpe, Lebo, Neodasha, Iola, Wamego, Osawatomie, Piqua, Oscaloosa and Neosho Rapids. He responded to these enlightenments by telling me the names of cities he had chosen to use in the dialogue of his vaudeville acts — Punxatawny, Scituate, Woosocket, Carnarsie, Manayunk, Kennebunkport. A further delight was the names he used in his films, such as Cuthbert J. Twilly, Hermisillo Brunch,

Larson E. Whipsnade, Felton J. Satchelstorm, Curtis I. Bascome, Dr. Otis Guelpe, Snerd Hearn, Figley E. Whiteside, and the fictitious law firm of Posthelwhistle and Smunn. He threw out a few more names which appealed to him. Charles Bogle, Otis Crimblecoblis, Mathatma Kane Jeeves.

The afternoon passed too quickly. At least, Mr. Fields didn't pay any attention to the heat and the delay of his call before the camera. But when, very late in the day, he was called for his scene, I thought the assistant director was going to kiss me!

Back in the publicity department, they looked upon me as a minor miracle, when I turned in twelve pages of text on W. C. Fields' life.

Thanks to Fields, his idle moments, and his penchant for words and names, I was launched on a publicist career. (It is being in the right place at the right time with the right idea and the right man needing the right ears of someone who has his or her own right needs.)

★　★　★

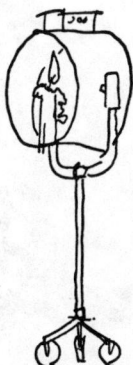

★ ★ ★

Another Bernie Kamins' tale to prove that publicists —
in the beginning of their professional lives, at least — don't
know *everything*! (Prior to his arrival in Hollywood, Bernie
was credited with concocting the story of Harvard students
swallowing live goldfish. It was heralded throughout the
nation.)

One of the mules of the *Hopalong Cassidy* production
was having a birthday, and someone on the set wondered
aloud what one should give a mule for a present.

Someone else suggested that a bale of alfalfa hay would
be appropriate. "Alfalfa" was a new word for Bernie and it
broke him up.

Then, he wrote a story under the by-line of the film's star,
William Boyd. He did not check out the story for
authenticity on "How To Take Care of Your Horse." In the
last paragraph, Bernie had Bill Boyd write:

> "If you're going to ride your horse, make sure that
> his feet are in good shape, or he can go
> permanently lame. Before you ride, lift each foot
> and see if there are any stones caught between his
> toes."

★ ★ ★

Publicists should always be wary, but never more so than when they are just beginning their professional duties. Especially publicists who work for film companies and television production units. One publicist learned some lessons when a story he wrote and released was picked up by a national wire service and saw print all over the country.

For one motion picture, a western being filmed at Columbia Pictures, director Ray Nazarro remembers that a member of the crew dreamed up an outlandish event and gave it to an unwary publicist. This variation of fun-and-games was given in all seriousness and with a straight face.

There was a sequence in which cattle — in the western film story — had to swim across a river, herded by a group of cowboys. The first assistant director told the neophyte unit publicist that what he couldn't see in the shot were the water wings the cattle were wearing. Water wings?

The first AD told the publicist that some cattle can't swim. It seemed that this was the case with this entire herd. The prop department had made 500 sets of giant water wings to help the cattle get across the river.

The young publicist did his duty and wrote the story. And it got printed!

★ ★ ★

Until well into the 1930s, the Associated Press had a rigid rule and would not use the title of a motion picture in any wire story. The reasoning was that a specific movie is a commodity, a product to be *sold* to a paying public. Like the brand name for a coffee, a candy bar, a laundry soap. In order to get the title of a picture published, the purveyor had to pay for an advertisement.

One now-forgotten publicist did have a moment of glory,

sneaking the title of the movie into an Associated Press story.

A western epic of the early Twenties was on location in the high mountain country of California when a freak snowstorm blew up and isolated the movie company for several days. The first stories used by the Associated Press referred only to "a movie on location." Then, one day, word of an attempt to solve the problem came down from the film location site. AP reported that a thundering herd of cattle was to be headed down the snow-blocked road in an effort to open it up and free the film company.

Much later, after the story had been picked up and widely printed by hundreds of newspapers, someone called to the attention of Associated Press editors that "a movie on location" was entitled *The Thundering Herd*.

★ ★ ★

Tremendous rivalry exists among publicity people. Those on a studio payroll work closely together for their common effort, the motion picture product.

Then there are the independent publicists, established to represent individuals, getting their clients' names in magazines and newspapers. One such publicist was independent Dave Epstein, who represented a writer or two. It was always difficult for writers to receive recognition in the press. Dave Epstein was an enterprising young man, well liked by the leading trade papers, *Variety* and *The Hollywood Reporter*. It is important that those two journals mention writers just to show how active they are.

Dave made up the name of a fictional Broadway stage producer — Ned Farrington. He was constantly getting stories published about one of his writer clients who was "asked by Ned Farrington to submit scripts" or stating that "Ned Farrington was interested in such-and-such a writer adapting his movie script for Broadway." The trade papers knew what Dave Epstein was doing, but went along with the Ned Farrington gag for a couple of years.

Then, Jim Henaghan, a reporter on *The Hollywood Reporter*, pulled a coup. Henaghan wrote a story that appeared in a Monday THR obituary column: the detailed account of the death of famous Broadway producer, Ned Farrington.

A still photographer and a publicist went with Gary Cooper to do a pictorial layout during a time he was appearing in a movie on location in the California lake country. Gary, an avid sportsman, wanted very much to make a catch. He was having no luck it seems — the fish avoided him.

Finally, as a gag, the publicist tore a bit of blue paper from the script Gary had with him. Grinning, Gary stuck a hook through it and cast out the line.

Bam! A healthy strike.

Actually, Cooper proved to have the biggest catch of the season on the end of his line. But who would believe it? Even the crew and the cast of the film production thought they were being duped.

Using a brand of "bait and switch," the publicist (who happened to be Teet Carle) got the story planted in a nearby city newspaper by telling the editor that Coop had made the record catch using a scrap of paper *torn from that newspaper's want-ad section.*

The story was printed front page.

★ ★ ★

George Glass wanted to get publicity for *Lady Godiva* a film about the noblewoman who had ridden a horse in public, clad only in her very lengthy flowing hair.

For George's stunt, he employed an aspiring (and uninhibited) actress, hired a horse, had flesh-colored tights fitted on the girl, and topped her off with a waist-length blonde wig. Boosting the actress aboard the nag, George started her riding up Hollywood Boulevard, expecting to attract maximum attention. His greatest hope was to get the *Godiva* girl arrested by the police, so that the incident would be covered by all the newspapers.

However, few pedestrians gave the girl more than a casual glance. When the horse and rider arrived at the corner of Hollywood and Vine, where a policeman was directing traffic, the beauty waved at the uniformed lawman. He smiled and waved back.

George Glass was frantic. Going up to the policeman he asked in an outraged tone, "Aren't you going to do something about that nude female?"

The policeman said no, he wasn't. But George kept at him until the man felt he'd been pestered enough.

"As far as I know," the policeman shouted at George, "there's no law against anyone riding a goddamn horse on Hollywood Boulevard. But it sure as hell is against the law to disturb the peace. If you don't shut up and get out of here, I'm going to take *you* in."

★ ★ ★

Clarence Locan, one publicist who could dream up some pretty unusual things, one day penned a story that star Maureen O'Sullivan had just received from a fan the smallest phonograph in the world; it measured only one inch by one inch, was completely workable, played records, and had excellent sound quality.

The story of Miss O'Sullivan's tiny phonograph was printed in many newspapers.

One day the MGM publicity department received a letter from the editors of *Popular Mechanics*, requesting a photograph of this smallest phonograph in the world.

Locan was on the spot — really in hot water! His co-workers backed off to watch him get out of it. It seemed certain his public lie would turn the tables on him. But Locan was a creative man. He assembled some pieces of cardboard, worked with some of the artisans of the studio property department, and came up with a beautiful little miniature phonograph. He had it photographed and sent the photo off to *Popular Mechanics*.

This most prestigious publication carried the picture on a full page.

"And the winner for the best publicity of the year is...."

★ ★ ★

During World War II, there were two photographs that were widely circulated. They are now collectors items.

One was of Betty Grable. She wore a one-piece swimsuit; in the shot she is looking back over her shoulder, her trim derriere cocked provocatively at the camera and the eye of the beholder.

The other photograph was of the feisty Carmen Miranda, taken during the filming of *Weekend in Havana* (starring John Payne, Alice Faye, and Cesar Romero). In a dance sequence, Cesar lifted Carmen high, her skirt billowing, her legs spread, her "nest" exposed as they passed before the still photographer, camera ready. He got the shot, and then he got fired!

The photographer took the negative with him. In just a short time those photographs of Betty Grable and Carmen Miranda found their way all over the world, showing up in strange places among the millions of American troops. But also in the bunkers of the appreciative Germans, Italians, and Japanese soldiers.

These comely girls showed the world — on both sides of the great conflict — the things that are really worth fighting for!

★ ★ ★

Publicity gimmicks often run in cycles. At times all the press agents in town begin vying with each other for some novelty to get attention for movies ready for press previews. If a movie has a western flavor, a publicity agent has been known to garb a lovely, leggy lady in short cowboy duds and send her out to hand deliver the invitations to screenings. To distribute invitations to a showing of *The Lady Eve*, Paramount promotion men dressed a nude cutie in a *papier mache* red apple!

There was one invitation gimmick that drew 100 percent complaints — for Warner's *Adventures of Robin Hood*. The press agent tied invitations to the shafts of arrows and hired a marksman with a sturdy bow to shoot the arrows into the front doors of the homes of press members all over the Hollywood area — Beverly Hills, Bel Air, Westwood, Encino, and points west!

It did not occur to the publicist who conceived the grand idea what an arrow could do to an oaken door. Studio carpenters were busy for weeks replacing front doors of angry members of the Fifth Estate!

★ ★ ★

It's funny how a novice publicist ends up being termed the "distinguished" public relations man of the community when he has barely survived all the tales that surround his early days and months. We promise this is the last Bernie Kamins yarn — but it is true!

Bernie Kamins felt he had to *experience* being a cowpoke (cowpike?) if he was going to be a good publicist for western stars and films. He wanted to learn to ride a horse. When the company he worked for went on location, Bernie told the wranglers that he desired more than anything, to be *one* of them — to learn *everything* they could teach him.

The wranglers were agreeable to the proposition. One of them, with a glint in his eye just short of a wink, asked Kamins if he would like to help in the "poling" of the hogs the next morning?

Of course, Bernie was *dee*lighted. And so at 4:00 A.M., Bernie was rousted out, driven to a ranch, and taken to the pigpen full of large hogs. Surrounding the hogpen were tall trees. Bernie was handed a long, stout pole. "This is what you pole the hogs with," the wrangler told him.

Bernie, to learn all of it, asked how do you pole the hog, and what was the reason he was doing this.

"These are oak trees," the wrangler said. "They're loaded with acorns, as you can see."

Bernie Kamins looked at the hogs in the pen, the oak trees standing nearby, the acorns hanging from the branches. He understood the lesson thus far.

"Now, the hogs love acorns," the wrangler said. "And they're very hungry. You see, you take this pole, and one by one, you stick it up a hog's ass, and hold him up so he can reach the acorns."

★ ★ ★

★ ★ ★

There was a veteran publicist at MGM in the 1930s and 1940s named Larry Barbier, who was noted as an expert troubleshooter. He enjoyed an excellent rapport with many of the studio's biggest stars, and they relied on him for advice and help whenever they found themselves in troublesome situations. Frequently the problems he had to deal with were private rather than public relations.

One morning he received an urgent call from Johnny Weissmuller, who was married to the volatile Lupe Velez. Johnny and Lupe were constantly having explosive arguments and fights, which were alternated with passionate reconciliations.

Larry rushed to their home, where he was admitted by a servant who directed him upstairs to a bedroom. Johnny and Lupe were still in bed, stark naked, and arguing furiously with each other.

Standing over them at the foot of the bed, the publicist was informed that he would have to mediate their dispute.

Larry agreed. "But you've got to calm down and talk rationally."

They agreed. "But you've got to get down on our level. Right now you're on a higher level and fully dressed."

Larry got undressed and climbed into bed to referee the fight.

VII
END CREDITS

"Tut, tut, my child," said the
Duchess. "Everything's got a
moral, if only you can find it."

★ ★ ★

Author and Publicist Will Fowler, the son of famed Hollywood writer and author Gene Fowler, was as a boy very close to comedian W. C. Fields. He even called Fields "Uncle Bill." Over the years, Will collected and filed many dozens of one-liners and sayings, which he has generously given us to share. Some of these "Fillosofies" of Fields are published for the first time.

For instance there is the one which might be true: "But then, Hollywood is a place that really never happened."

About the breaking of wind: "Most people are secretive about it. Of course, a burglar has to be!"

Referring once to movie producers, Fields expounded: "I grow the trees, and they want to pick the fruit."

It can be noted that "When a man is beside himself, he's in bad company."

★ ★ ★

One day Steve McQueen asked: "If President Jimmy Carter's Chief of Staff calls himself Hamilton Jurdon, shouldn't the Press Secretary be called Jurdy Purl?"

★ ★ ★

When *Hair*, one of the first Broadway productions to feature nudity, played to capacity, someone asked Groucho Marx if he had seen it.

"No," Groucho said with a straight face. "I saved twelve bucks by going back to the hotel, taking off my clothes, and looking at myself in the mirror."

★ ★ ★

"Birth is the Fourth of July of sex."
— *W. C. Fields*

At one time it wasn't common knowledge that James Cagney is a fine painter. One evening a writer went to Cagney's home to interview him; while waiting for the actor's appearance, the writer became intrigued by the western oil painting hanging over the mantelpiece. The writer was an avid admirer of the works of Remington and of Charles Russell, both of whom were renowned for artfully depicting the historical West in fine paintings.

When James Cagney entered the room, the writer told him he envied him the Charles Russell painting.

"No," Jimmy said. "That's not a Russell. It's a Cagney."

★ ★ ★

Will Fowler has laughingly described an incident when John D. Rockefeller, Jr., visited some of his money in Hollywood.

Young Rockefeller placed a telephone call from a booth (when a coin call was still a nickel). Failing to reach his party, he hung up the phone, but the nickel wasn't returned. He got the operator back on the line and reported his loss. She asked him for his name and address, telling him his nickel would be returned by mail.

"Oh, forget it," Rockefeller replied. "You wouldn't believe it if I told you."

Another gem from W. C. Fields: "Words of malice always spring from envy."

Production manager and assistant director Francisco "Chico" Day, recalls William Dieterle, Hungarian film director, during the filming of *Omar Khayyam* (which starred Cornel Wilde and Debra Paget).

Dieterle's accent was thick with the mixture of East European and American idioms. Once, setting up for a scene, he looked through the view-finder attached to the camera, at the same time calling out to two male actors, telling them where he wanted them to stand and what he expected them to do.

"Joe, you go on 'action'," he said in his heavy accent, and employing hand motions. "And then, Pete, you come on my hand."

For many years, all Warners pictures bore the trademark of a shield featuring the label "Warner Bros."

One day a nice-looking man showed up at the company's New York offices, announcing that he wanted to have an appointment with the story editor. "I'm an intimate friend of your head man," he told the receptionist.

He was asked, "Who might that be?"

"Why, Mr. Bros, of course."

As with the previous story, it is best that this tale not carry the names of the individuals involved.

A female star, high on the charts in self-centeredness, fell in love with the quite handsome director of the film in which she was appearing. There began a romance that resulted in her plea for them to marry.

The director reported that he had asked his wife of twenty years to divorce him, but she had refused him.

"How dare that woman!" the actress raged. "How dare she stand in the way of *my* happiness."

★ ★ ★

"I once knew a poor soul who blew his booze money on the rent."
— *W. C. Fields*

★ ★ ★

When discussing politics, and in reference to a potential candidate for President of the United States, W. C. Fields asked the question: "Would America settle for an intellectual gelding?"

★ ★ ★

While not truly a Hollywood story except for the appearance of opera star and motion picture actor, William Chapman, it should be recorded that when he appeared with famed diva Beverly Sills in the opera *Tosca*, the expected turned into the unexpected.

The scene being sung with all the usual frenzies that opera demands called for Miss Sills to kill Mr. Chapman by stabbing. For the performances, Bill had constructed a "cackle-bladder," a container filled with a gooey bloodlike substance, which would pour forth and cling to his white shirt when he was struck on the chest with the rubber knife.

When the scene was done, Bill squeezed the cackle-bladder. Instead of just breaking and covering him with the red goo, it burst out in several directions, hitting Beverly Sills in the face, spraying out over the orchestra in the pit, and even reaching some of the front seats of the audience.

Maintaining tremendous composure, Beverly wiped the "blood" out of her eyes and from her face. Delivering her next line caused the dramatic moment to convulse the cast, orchestra, audience, and Mr. Chapman.

"Let your own blood choke you!" she trilled.

★ ★ ★

★ ★ ★

Groucho Marx made application for membership in a certain highly-restricted private club. He was notified — as cautiously as possible — that the club could not accept any members who were Jewish.

"I primarily was interested in my daughter using the swimming pool," Groucho instantly responded. "She's only half-Jewish. Can she go in the pool only up to her waist?"

Marx later was heard to make the remark, "I would never join a club that would accept *me* as a member."

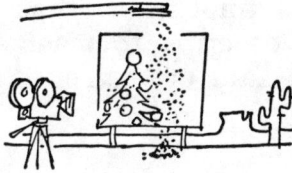

The oft-married Gabor sisters have been in the news for many years, and they continue to peal out oneliners that afford them space in the columns.

Eva Gabor, according to the *Los Angeles Times*, gave a talk before a group of 400 women who were doctors' wives. She discoursed on her various acting roles, related her wifely experiences and attitudes, and discussed her businesses. During the question-and-answer session that followed, she was asked by one of the ladies present: "If a woman breaks off an engagement, should she return the ring?"

"Return the ring," Eva briskly responded. "But keep the stone."

★ ★ ★

★ ★ ★

Errol Flynn, rarely allowing a female to slip by unappreciated, interviewed a strikingly beautiful woman to handle publicity and public relations for him. Just to be sure not to pass up anything, Flynn made a pass at the lady.

"Mr. Flynn," she responded with a smile. "You may hire me, or you can keep me. But not both."

He saved himself the money. He hired her.

★ ★ ★

At one point or another in their careers, actors are always asked to describe themselves. Basil Rathbone (Sherlock Holmes) said of himself: "I resemble a folded umbrella."

★ ★ ★

Bing Crosby and Phil Harris, the bandleader whose name is associated with many stories connected with drink and drinking, were slated to share an event in Kansas City. Phil stopped off to visit relatives en route. Bing arrived alone in the midwestern city. A woman reporter interviewed him for a local paper. "But why is Mr. Harris not with you?"

"He'll be here tomorrow," said Crosby. "He had to stop off in Kentucky to place a wreath on the grave of Jack Daniels!"

★ ★ ★

Sam Goldwyn created some of the greatest motion pictures in the century. He never did anything small, and all he touched became greater. He will be remembered for what he has accomplished more than for what he has said. Goldwyn did, however, have a distinct language. Having produced *The Best Years Of Our Lives* he told a news interviewer, "I don't care if this film makes a dime or not so long as everyone in the country goes in to see it."

★ ★ ★

In the early years of the film industry's talking pictures Arthur Caesar took every opportunity to uphold his position as the kingpin among movietown's wits and funny men. Once he had a make-up artist apply a full-blooming black eye to his face. Then Caesar had a still photographer shoot a close-up portrait of the black-eyed face.

He sent one print to Darryl Zanuck. Arthur Caesar inscribed the portrait: "Nobody can talk that horribly about you when I'm around!"

★ ★ ★

★ ★ ★

There is a story told about Jerry Wald, producer of some extraordinary fare who ultimately ended up at 20th Century-Fox. Wald spoke at a press conference, referring to his current picture, and naming several other known and unknown accomplishments of his past pictures.

"He's not as conceited as I've been told he is," one reporter said to another reporter, at the end of the conference.

"But he does seem to have a lot to be modest about," the other reporter replied.

★ ★ ★

Star comedian George Gobel once asked, "Have you ever had a feeling that the world is a tuxedo and you are a pair of brown shoes?"

★ ★ ★

Once during a press conference, Groucho Marx was asked how things had changed since the generation when he was getting started in show business.

"They called us the Lost Generation," was Groucho's immediate reply. "This generation today hasn't even been lost so it can be found!"

★ ★ ★

"When doctors and undertakers meet they always wink at each other."
— W. C. Fields

★ ★ ★

Self-centeredness is a disease to which all stars — no matter their background or personalities — seem to fall victim to some extent. To those who have worked with the actors and actresses of movieland, Hedda Hopper's story is really just another "the-show-must-go-on" tale, and therefore can be understood with some compassion.

Norma Shearer and her husband, Irving Thalberg, were best friends of Douglas Fairbanks and his then wife, Lady Sylvia Ashley. Miss Shearer arranged a dinner party at her home for the Fairbanks and their most intimate friends. However, Mrs. Fairbanks called before dinner to cancel. Douglas was ill.

During the dinner, Miss Shearer's butler approached her as she sat at the head of the table and whispered to her. Momentarily, Miss Hopper reported, Norma Shearer paled, but then composed herself, and the dinner continued. After dinner, dancing and games made it a gala affair until the wee hours of the morning. It was not until the guests left that they learned Fairbanks had died at 9:30 P.M.

Hedda Hopper asked Norma Shearer later how she could have kept quiet when she knew her guests were Douglas Fairbanks' best friends.

"What else could I do?" the popular star replied. "I couldn't say anything — it would have spoiled my party."

★ ★ ★

Many tales have attempted to reveal the inner Gary Cooper. It's told that Gary's doctor knew the actor had cancer. Although he had not informed Cooper, the doctor had told Gary's wife Rocky and the family.

One day Rocky found Gary in the den polishing a hunting rifle. She asked Cooper what he was planning to do.

"I'm getting restless," Gary replied. "I think I'll go on a hunt somewhere."

Rocky called the doctor, and an appointment was made for Gary Cooper to have a talk with the medic. At the meeting, Gary was informed of his condition; he had terminal cancer, and his days were numbered. After a moment, Gary spoke kindly to his doctor. "Gosh," he is said to have commented. "I feel sorry for you, Doc. It must be horrible to have to tell a patient he's dying."

Shortly thereafter he was talking with his friend, Ernest Hemingway. Over the telephone lines he talked with "Papa" Hemingway about the news he had received. Hemingway also suffered with cancer and knew it. "Well, Pops," Gary remarked. "I'm going to beat you to the corral."

★ ★ ★

There was once a touring Hollywood medicine man who guaranteed to grow hair on any naked head. He offered $100 to men who would complete his course of twelve treatments and not grow hair.

The victim paid $10 up front for treatments. The "doctor" administered the first one which, it is said, consisted of massaging the bare scalp with a fine steel brush. Then a turpentine shampoo was applied, vigorously worked into the scalp.

No patron ever returned to receive the other eleven treatments.

★ ★ ★

Some very colorful ladies and gentlemen represented the entertainment sections of newspapers in cities throughout the nation. From time to time, they would descend on Hollywood to visit the stars, gather materials to ballyhoo the films being produced, and write about great parties and industry events for the edification of their readers. One such delight was Fairfax Nesbit, drama writer and critic with the *Dallas Morning News.*

Fairfax Nesbit (the name is *real*) hailed originally from Georgia. Her very pronounced southern drawl combined with the Texas twang. No one in America spoke like Fairfax Nesbit.

One warm sunny day, Miss Nesbit checked into the Hollywood Roosevelt Hotel and rang for the bellhop to take her clothes out for pressing.

The bellhop, a Filipino lad, had been in America only six months. "Pullleezzee hav' these clo'es praay'ussd," Fairfax instructed the young man.

The bellhop withdrew quickly and ran down to the front desk for help. "There is a foreign woman in 309," he said. "She can't speak the Eengleesh."

Very prominent in the credits of every motion picture is the name of its producer. In fact, many films have a number of producers' names, of varying levels. The producers are, of course, among the most powerful of people in Hollywood, and during the golden era of the studios, they wielded their power unchallenged. People could be hired or fired at their whims. Some of them had brothers or in-laws or cousins placed on payrolls in various capacities.

Once Fred Allen was asked, "What do producers produce?"

The comedian replied, "Relatives."

★ ★ ★

At his best, Fred Allen was one of the funniest of comedians. He was at his best one evening in 1951, when the Friars Club gave a testimonial dinner for Jack Benny. He was brilliant; every line had the assembled guests roaring with laughter. When he had finished, he received a standing ovation.

It was one of those moments that all public figures dread. Allen's was not the final speech of the evening, and it would really take something special to follow him.

The person scheduled to speak next was Governor Adlai Stevenson of Illinois, who would become the Democratic nominee for President the following year.

As he was being introduced, Stevenson had to think fast. Standing before the gathering, he improvised, saying, "When I arrived here tonight, I met Fred Allen in the lobby. He was very despondent because he had prepared nothing to say. I did not want Fred to be a flop before this illustrious assemblage, so I gave him my speech to deliver. Now, I just want to thank you for the wonderful reception you've given to it."

He sat down, also to a standing ovation.

★ ★ ★

Jack Elam,the ever popular character actor, enjoys practical jokes. One he developed involves putting some warm water in a small Dixie cup, hiding it within a handkerchief, then pretending he has a cold. When standing close to someone, he presumably blows his nose, at the same time flicking water from the cup with his fingers. Drops of spray filter onto the person standing nearby.

A young blonde girl — an extra, new to filmdom and practical jokers — was on a set one day. Jack caught her with his watery snozzling a number of times. In an effort to be diplomatic, the girl tried to stay away from him, but Elam kept following her about.

In desperation, the girl found an umbrella. Everytime Jack raised his handkerchief, the blonde girl opened the umbrella between them.

★ ★ ★

Some stories never get into print because truth is stranger than fiction. Some stories are just too good to *be* true! One of the most famous stories happened at MGM, during preparation to make author L. Frank Baum's immortal *The Wizard of Oz*.

Actor Frank Morgan, cast as the Wizard, was being tested in various wardrobe changes. Mary Mayer, the unit publicist assigned to the picture, came into the publicity department that day bubbling over with a coincidence story.

In the wardrobe department, Frank Morgan had been trying on some old, heavy, frayed overcoats to select one to wear in the picture. As he was replacing a coat on the rack, his eye fell on the label.

Frank called it to the attention of the wardrobe and camera people who were present:

"Made in Chicago for L. Frank Baum."

Mary Mayer telephoned Baum's widow and asked about the coat. Yes, Mrs. Baum remembered the coat.

When the Baums had moved to Hollywood, they brought along all their clothing. However, no longer needing a heavy woolen winter coat in the land of the sun, Frank had given the coat, along with other midwest winter clothing, to charity. Somehow it had found its way into the MGM wardrobe.

It was agreed that the press editors and reporters would never believe such a story. It never saw print.

Until now.

★ ★ ★

North of Los Angeles, on a hill just outside of Newhall, California, sits a white castle-like structure. Here the owner of that castle and the many acres that surround it, William S. Hart, earliest of western screen stars, lived out the last decades of his life.

From the year 1914 until the mid-1920s, Hart earned great sums of tax-free money as a top movie star. When oil was discovered in the vicinity of his ranch and castle, Hart refused all offers to grant mineral and drilling rights. He said he would not permit the oil derricks to spoil the natural beauty of that place.

William S. Hart died without family (in his younger years he had been married for a short time) and his will left everything to Los Angeles County. His reason: "The public gave it all to me by paying to see my pictures; I want to give it back to them."

★ ★ ★

$\star$ $\star$ $\star$

Every actor and technician who has worked in "live" television productions has stories about things that went wrong and had to be covered up before the millions of viewers.

In a live performance of the television series *Mystery Is My Hobby*, leading actor Glenn Langan and his leading lady were in a decrepit old cabin out in the boondocks, looking for murder clues. The set and props consisted of a potbellied stove, with coffee pot, a pump in the sink, assorted cutlery on the wooden sink top, a rickety old table, and a couple of chairs.

The door swung open, and an evil looking "heavy" entered, pointing a .45 caliber pistol. Glenn remarked that the mystery was now clear, that he (the heavy with gun) was the killer. To the leading lady, he added that the killer was probably a coward and would not shoot them. Whereupon Mr. Killer took aim at the coffee pot and pulled off a shot.

At this point, a stagehand was supposed to pull a string attached to the pot and jerk if off the stove. The pot remained where it was.

"You're not a very good shot," Glenn sneeringly ad-libbed.

The heavy became quite nervous. "Yeah?" he said. "Well, watch this." He aimed and pulled off another shot.

This time the stagehand did his job and pulled the string. The coffee pot teetered, but the string broke and the pot remained upright.

The studio audience began to giggle. Frantic now, the killer pulled the trigger once more. The gun clicked. Then it clicked again. Being a good actor, the heavy hurled the useless piece to the floor and scooped up a butcher knife lying on the kitchen sink. "I'm going to stab you," he warned Glenn.

The two actors closed and waltzed until they thought they were in a camera position where Glenn could be "knifed," whereupon he fell to the floor, dead!

At that moment, the door flung open and two armed policemen entered. One pointed to Glenn. "He's been shot," he said, following the original script.

"No, he's been stabbed," the leading lady corrected.

The lawman looked confused. "But, we heard shots!"

The lady, suppressing hysteria, sought for a reasonable way to alter the script. "Well, you see, it's like this," she said. "The killer is a very bad shot, and he had to use a knife."

An afterword: Glenn Langan has said to several friends that if, at that moment, the camera had moved in for a close-up of him, it would have been on a corpse trying desperately not to laugh.

★ ★ ★

"I've screwed myself out of fortunes; Most guys have screwed themselves into them."
— *W. C. Fields*

★ ★ ★

The most earth-shaking scene in the motion picture, *It Happened One Night*, was not the one in which Claudette Colbert showed Clark Gable how to hitchhike a ride by pulling her skirt up to show a stockinged leg all the way to her upper thigh. It was a scene that followed.

In the motel, Claudette and Clark share a room. With separate beds, of course. Gable pulls off his shirt exposing a bare torso — not covered with *an undershirt*!

The men's undershirt manufacturers suffered the biggest plummet in the history of haberdashery.

★ ★ ★

★ ★ ★

When hard-boiled novelist James Cain was writing for the screen, he told the story of a glamorous woman author who made a bundle of money from her best-selling novel. The story was sprinkled with sex, mild by today's explicit details of fornications. The lady, with all her gains, proceeded to make good on a long-nurtured dream of having her boudoir all in yellow — the walls, the draperies, the carpeting, the bedding and furnishings.

Despite the redesigning, the repainting, and the refurbishing, the lady fell ill. She came down with yellow jaundice, and a doctor was called in.

One gossip wag reported to her readers that the lady nearly died before the doctor was able to find her!

In 1933 Norman Krasna was at Columbia Pictures. Krasna and his chief, Harry Cohn, had been in a war of sorts over a raise in pay — Krasna's raise in pay, of course.

On the day of the famous 5:55 P.M. Long Beach earthquake that jolted all of southern California, Krasna reached for his telephone and got directly through to the studio head. "Mr. Cohn," Krasna said in deep sonorous tones. "This is God. That was a warning to do right for Krasna — or a bigger warning will follow."

★ ★ ★

★ ★ ★

In September 1961, making a film in the Sacramento area, the French star Maurice Chevalier celebrated his eightieth birthday. The cast and crew hosted a luncheon for him. Gilbert Lee Kay enthused to Maurice during lunch, "Isn't it wonderful! You've done it! You look marvelous. How does it feel to reach eighty?"

Chevalier turned on his smile and his ineffable charm. "Not bad when you consider the alternative," he said.

★ ★ ★

Back in the lush, plush days of Hollywood, when blonde comedienne star Marion Davies was the mistress of a huge house on the Santa Monica beach, she hosted parties to which hundreds were invited. Other live-in dozens had their own rooms or apartments contained within the giant complex. When Marion finally divested herself of the property, national columnist Florabel Muir wrote of the cataclysmic event:

MARION DAVIES CLOSES BEACH HOUSE.
THOUSANDS HOMELESS.

★ ★ ★

"He has delusions of humility."
— *W. C. Fields*

★ ★ ★

★ ★ ★

Beatrice Lillie, the great British comedienne of stage and screen, was also Lady Peel, a titled member of British gentry. During a period between pictures, she appeared in a Broadway stage show playing herself, as "Lady Peel."

In one scene, the actor playing opposite her, in a teatime sequence, rang for the butler, and then decomposed his next line:

"Please bring Lady Teel's pee."

★ ★ ★

Index

"Oomph Girl, The," 12
Orr, Clifford, 133
Orr, William, 59
Osawatomie, 146
Oscaloosa, 146
O'Sullivan, Maureen, 152-154
Our Gang kids, 60

Pacoima, 146
Paget, Debra, 164
Panama Canal, 48
Pantages, Alexander, 57-58
Pantages Theater, 58
Paramount Pictures, 8, 13, 15, 21,
    25, 31, 38, 41, 44, 54, 73, 75, 78,
    81, 85-86, 88, 91, 93-96, 98, 107-
    108, 114, 126, 129, 137, 139, 142,
    145, 155
Paramount Ranch, 44
Parker, Dorothy, 129, 133
Parnell, 16
Parsons, Louella, 140
Pasadena Playhouse, 25, 27-28
Payne, John, 154
Peck, Gregory, 82
Peel, Lady, 182
Pegler, Westbrook, 132
Perry Mason, 101
Pershing, Gen. John, 26-27
Pickford, Mary, 54
Pine, William, 139
Pine-Thomas, 57
Piqua, 146
"Platinum Blonde, The," 12
Point Magu, 146
Pomona, 146
Pons, Lilly, 53
Poppea, 91
Poppy, 145
Popular Mechanics, 154
Porter, Cole, 11
Portland, Oregon, 41
Postelwhistle and Smunn, 147
Powell, Dick, 102
Powell, Jody, 161
Powell, William, 64
Preston, Robert, 26-27

Pringle, Aileen, 75
Producers' Studios, 34
Punxatawny, 146

RKO Studios, 10, 53, 93
Rainer, Luise, 63-64
Ralston, Esther, 15
Rank, J. Arthur, 26
Rathbone, Basil, 94, 168
Reagan, Ronald, 37
Remarque, Erich Maria, 79
Remington, Frederick, 162
Republic Studios, 58, 83
Reseda, 146
Reynolds, Burt, 11
Rhubarb, 129-130
Rich, Frank, 11
Richards, Addison, 89
Roach, Hal, 60
Rockefeller, John D. Jr., 164
Rodgers, Richard, 81
Rogers, Roy, 83
Rome, Italy, 107
Romero, Cesar, 154
Rooney, Mickey, 34
Running Wild, 145
Russell, Charles, 162
Russell, Jane, 10
Russell, Rosalind, 16, 71-72,
    94-96

Sacramento, 181
Sally of the Sawdust, 145
Samson, 82
San Bernardino, 49
Sands Hotel, 96
San Fernando Valley, 44-45, 101,
    145
San Francisco, 137
Santa Monica Boulevard, 106
Santa Monica Mountains, 106
Satchelstorm, Felton J., 147
Saturday Evening Post, The, 111
Saturday Review, 119
Schafer, Adolph L. "Whitey,"
    40, 98
Schroeder, Carl, 82